There is no topic more urgent for our time, especially in the current political climate of the U.S., than migration. And there is no one more qualified to write on it than Dr. Nguyễn, himself a refugee from Vietnam and a New Testament scholar. His passion for justice and his love for migrants and refugees make the teaching of the Bible on strangers, migrants, and refugees come alive. I most enthusiastically recommend this book not only to those responsible for public policies for immigration but also to the migrants themselves.

Peter C. Phan, The Ignacio Ellacuria Chair of Catholic Social Thought, Georgetown University

This book is compelling, informative, and challenging. Nguyễn addresses several of the tragic examples of rootlessness in today's world and thoughtfully describes the plight of the victims of such evils. He draws parallels with comparable situations found within the biblical story and then underscores how that same religious tradition called God's people in the past and us in the present to remedy such evils. This informative book lends itself to serious personal reflection as well as challenging group discussion.

Dianne Bergant, CSA, Distinguished Professor Emerita of Old Testament Studies, Catholic Theological Union

This book is a gem. In an accessible style, Nguyễn deftly connects the varied and complex realities of modern migration with biblical texts that reflect similar experiences. This little volume demonstrates that the Scripture can speak to the plights of today's sociopolitical and climate refugees, asylum seekers, the slave trade, and others on the move around the globe. Nguyễn also brings Catholic teaching into the discussion, but it would be a shame to limit its audience to readers of that tradition. There is much here for all Christians!

M. Daniel Carroll R., Scripture Press Ministries
Professor of Biblical Studies and Pedagogy,
Wheaton College

The book skillfully weaves migration stories and themes in the Bible with the challenges of human mobility in the twenty-first century. Its attention to the breadth and complexity of the migration experience, exploration of lesser-known biblical texts, highly-accessible language, and practical approach makes it a refreshing and rewarding read. It is most certainly a valuable contribution to the burgeoning literature on migration theologies.

Gemma Tulud Cruz, Senior Lecturer in Theology,
Australian Catholic University

What Does
the Bible
Say About... **?**

Strangers,
Migrants,
and Refugees

"What Does the Bible Say About...?" Series
Ronald D. Witherup, P.S.S.
Series Editor

What Does
the Bible
Say About... **?**

Strangers,
Migrants,
and Refugees

vănThanh Nguyễn, S.V.D.

New City Press

Hyde Park, New York

Published by New City Press
202 Comforter Blvd.,
Hyde Park, NY 12538
www.newcitypress.com

©2021 New City Press

Cover design and layout by Miguel Tejerina
Illustration by Route55/Dreamstime.com

Biblical citations are taken from the New Revised Standard Version
©1989 Division of Christian Education of the National Council of the
Churches of Christ in the United States of America.
Library of Congress Cataloging-in-Publication Data

What does the Bible say about Strangers, Migrants, and Refugees

Library of Congress Control Number: 2020952654

ISBN: 978-1-56548-376-7
ISBN: 978-1-56548-377-4 (e-book)
ISBN: 978-1-56548-697-3 (series ISBN)

Printed in the United States of America

Contents

To Stan Uroda, SVD,
a generous confrere, dear friend,
and gracious missionary

Series Preface

The Bible remains the world's number one best-seller of all time. Millions of copies in more than two thousand languages and dialects are sold every year, yet how many are opened and read on a regular basis? Despite the impression the Bible's popularity might give, its riches are not easy to mine. Its message is not self-evident and is sometimes hard to relate to our daily lives.

This series addresses the need for a reliable guide to reading the Bible profitably. Each volume is designed to unlock the Bible's mysteries for the interested reader who asks, "What does the Bible say about…?" Each book addresses a timely theme in contemporary culture, based upon questions people are asking today, and explaining how the Bible can speak to these questions as reflected in both Old and New Testaments.

Ideal for individual or group study, each volume consists of short, concise chapters on a biblical theme in non-technical language, and in a style accessible to all. The expert authors have been chosen for their knowledge of the Bible. While taking into account current scholarship, they know how to explain the Bible's teaching in simple language. They are also able to relate the biblical message to the challenges of today's Church and society while avoiding a simplistic use of the biblical text for trying to "prove" a point or defend a position, which is called "prooftexting"—an improper use of the Bible. The focus in these books is on a religious perspective, explaining what the Bible says, or does not say, about each theme. Short discussion questions invite sharing and reflection.

So, take up your Bible with confidence, and with your guide explore "what the Bible says about STRANGERS, MIGRANTS, AND REFUGEES."

Introduction

Have you ever wondered what it's like to be an immigrant living in a foreign land or a refugee fleeing from war, violence, or natural disaster? I know, for I am one. Being an immigrant and a refugee was not easy, but it has taught me many lessons. One is the importance of being in solidarity with the millions of people who are displaced all over the globe. Although my parents originally came from North Viet Nam, I was actually born and raised in the South of my homeland. After the Fall of Saigon in 1975, my family and I emigrated to the United States of America as refugees, seeking religious freedom and other basic human rights that were no longer available under the communist political regime. My family certainly knows what it's like to be stripped of all fundamental human rights, especially the freedoms of expression and worship. To live under such oppressive conditions was not an option for committed Christians. We preferred to die together at sea in a flimsy boat, seeking "a new heaven and a new earth" (Revelation 21:1) and taking our chances with nature, rather than to live facing death from hunger and deprived of faith and hope.

The migrant and refugee crisis has erupted enormously and has become one of the major factors shaping the world today. On the highways and byways of every continent, millions of people are constantly on the move. In the last several decades, the number of people on the move has increased exponentially. By mid-year 2020, it was estimated that approximately 3.4 percent of the world's 7.6 billion people were displaced. That's one out of every thirty people on the planet now living away from his or her homeland. From another perspective, if migrants and refugees were gathered in one place, they would constitute the fifth largest nation on earth, surpassing forty-five million more than the whole population of the country of Brazil. According to the International Organization of Migration (IOM), it is projected that by 2050 there could be as many as 405 million international migrants globally.[1]

Because of the growing inequalities of wealth caused by globalization, political and ethnic conflicts, environmental disasters, virus pandemics (like COVID-19), free trade, and viable means of transportation, more and more people are migrating than ever before, causing some to call our era "the age of migration."

Migration is by no means a new phenomenon. Since the dawn of human history, wave upon wave of people have been on the move for a variety of reasons, including trade, war, persecution, natural disasters, economic opportunities, asylum, and even adventure. Interestingly, the Bible contains many stories written by, for, and about strangers, migrants, and refugees. It begins with the first human parents banished from Paradise and ends with the prophet John exiled on the island of Patmos. Encapsulated between these two bookends, namely Genesis and Revelation, are stories of God's people constantly on the move. Thus, we could correctly say that the Bible is essentially a tapestry woven together from the stories of one huge migrant family. Since these sacred texts are written by, for, and about migrants, it is worthwhile to examine some of its key figures and events in order to draw out appropriate responses to one of the most challenging phenomena of our time—migration.

Crossing international borders, or even moving around within a country, is a major characteristic of our present age. No continent, region, or country is immune from this worldwide phenomenon. Recognizing the complexities and concerns of the plight of millions still in desperate circumstances, this book seeks to develop an appropriate response from each person and the worldwide community to this phenomenon. Since the Bible is the Word of God and the basis of our faith and practice, we will turn to the Christian Scriptures to search for inspiration and guidance. The aim is to provide a biblical basis and framework to address the issues of migration today.

Chapter One

"Life is but a Sojourn"

Plato once said, "Life is but a sojourn." There is a lot of truth in this philosophical statement. I was born into a family that was constantly on the move. Rooting and uprooting happened multiple times in my early childhood. For some people, this might sound intriguing or even idyllic. However, when you are an immigrant running away from war or natural disaster in order to survive, life can be extremely difficult and is often painful. The most heart wrenching experience for me was being on a boat drifting at sea for seven days. We were exposed to the elements of nature. Food was scarce. Drinking water was carefully rationed. Although I was only a child then, I could still feel the pain and suffering all around me. Besides being hungry and thirsty, I became homeless and stateless. I understood then that my life would never be the same again. This new reality frightened me and caused me deep sorrow, as if I had been swept over by a tidal wave.

Life as an immigrant is no joke! An immigrant is vulnerable, relying always on the generosity of others and on the whims of nature. Realizing that life is but a sojourn should cause us to be more sympathetic with those immigrants who are displaced from their home and trapped at the borders.

Israel's Ancestors as Immigrants

The Bible addresses this issue explicitly. The first eleven chapters of the book of Genesis are filled with stories of forced and voluntary migration. Due to pride and selfishness, namely wanting to be like God, Adam and Eve disobeyed God's commands and consequently were expelled from the Garden of Eden (Genesis 3:16-24). They barely had time to enjoy the fruits and sanctuary of Paradise provided by God. Interestingly, however, before the first parents were exiled to earth to secure their own shelter and till the land for food, God showed deep affection and concern for these earliest sojourners by sewing skins together to clothe them and protect them from the elements (Genesis 3:21).

The theme of alienation and displacement continues with Cain who kills his brother Abel out of jealousy (Genesis 3:8-16). As a punishment, he becomes a fugitive and wanderer on the earth. Despite Cain's hideous act of cruelty, God still cares for this criminal vagrant by placing a mark of protection on him so that no one would kill him. As the inhabitants of the earth increase, wickedness, violence, and degradation of the earth sickens God to the point of regret for having created humanity. Thus, God purges the earth and all its inhabitants with a huge flood. Noah and his family, who were righteous before God and chosen to continue the human race, were forced to flee their land because of this tragedy. Like many victims of natural disasters, they became immigrants without a known destination. Nevertheless, trusting in the covenant promised by God, Noah sails over the waves of fear and chaos to find a new home on a distant shore (Genesis 6:18). But that is not the end! The Tower of Babel presents another tale about forced migration. In this story, the whole of humanity decides to challenge God by constructing a tower that would reach heaven. For their sin of pride, God confuses the language of all the inhabitants and scatters them throughout the face of the earth (Genesis 11:1-9).

In short, the first eleven chapters of the book of Genesis recount tales of the earliest human families as migrants and refugees, moving about the earth seeking a land to settle and a home in which to dwell. They risked everything for a better life. What is most noticeable in these accounts is that God cares for and protects these fugitives, vagrants, or immigrants despite their shortcomings.

Israel's ancestral history really begins with Abraham and Sarah when they responded to God's uncertain promises and invitation to leave their familiar surroundings in Mesopotamia (literally "between the two rivers," Tigris and Euphrates) and to sojourn to the land of Canaan (Genesis 12:9). While they were still wandering about searching for a dwelling, a famine broke out in the land forcing them to flee to Egypt and reside there as "aliens" (Genesis 12:10). After finding refuge in Egypt, they continued to wander about aimlessly in the Negeb (a semi-desert area located in the southern part of today's Israel-Palestine) to Bethel and then to Ai (Genesis 13:1-3). Eventually Abraham and his clan pitched their tents at Mamre near Hebron as their principal place of residence but only for a time, because their journey did not end there. As nomads, Abraham and his kinsfolk continued to move about in Canaan searching for food and pasture for their livestock. They seemed to have finally settled in Beer-sheba (Genesis 21:33), but it is interesting to note that at the death of Sarah, Abraham had to purchase a burial place for her and for himself in the cave of the field of Machpelah (Genesis 23:19). This is a clear indication that even until the very end of their earthly existence Abraham and Sarah never ceased being strangers and sojourners in the land of promise.

The same is true with Isaac and Rebekah, as well as with Jacob and his two wives Leah and Rachel. While Isaac's primary domicile was at Beer-sheba and Jacob's at Shechem, each also moved about with his flocks and herds, not attached to any particular place. Eventually, one of Jacob's twelve sons, Joseph, was sold into slavery in Egypt because of sibling rivalry. The dramatic epic of Joseph's displacement and rise to power in Egypt sets the stage for Israel's massive migration to the land of the Pharaohs where they are saved from a terrible famine in Palestine and eventually become permanent resident aliens.

Israel's memory of their founding ancestors is fundamentally as *gerim*,[2] a Hebrew designation that can loosely be translated as resident aliens, strangers, sojourners, or (more appropriately) immigrants. Abraham even described himself as an immigrant or *ger*, which is a singular form of the plural noun *gerim* (Genesis 23:4). In Exodus 6:4 the patriarchs are referred to collectively as *gerim* when God declares to Moses that he had promised to give them the land in which they were dwelling as outsiders. Even the psalmist refers to Abraham, Isaac, and Jacob as *gerim* who wandered about Canaan before their descendants took possession of the land at a later time (Psalm 105:8-13). And in two other instances, Psalm 39:13 and First Chronicles 29:15, Israel's fathers are called *gerim*. Not surprisingly, the Israelites were commanded to always remember their sojourning heritage when they enter the Promised Land and harvest the fruits of the earth. They are to recall, saying, "My father was a refugee Aramean who went down to Egypt with a small household and lived there as a resident alien. But there he became a nation great, strong and numerous" (Deuteronomy 26:5, NABRE).

We learn from these ancestral stories that God encounters and calls people who are less than perfect and frequently on the run. They are often not the best of characters. Some are not even honest. Jacob, for example, was a deceiver and schemer; yet God chose him and placed him in the line of promise. Even though these *immigrants* are vulnerable, frail, and even sinful, they are not nameless and faceless but rather are created *in the image and likeness of God.* They are human beings and should be treated with the dignity that has been divinely bestowed upon them. Often, those who show kindness to these folks do not go unnoticed but are rewarded abundantly. Consequently, biblical writers continue to remind their readers to treat the strangers and immigrants in their midst with respect and dignity (Exodus 22:20; 23:9; Leviticus 19:33-34; Deuteronomy 5:15; 10:19), for to neglect the needs of these vulnerable migrants makes one liable to punishment (Deuteronomy 24:14-15).

Migration – A Global Phenomenon

It is said that migration is as old as history. While migration is certainly not a new phenomenon, it is nonetheless a major crisis of our epoch. Every day millions of people are relentlessly on the move. Some travel for the purpose of tourism. Others do it for business. Many, however, migrate because of political, economic, and ecological reasons.

Migration may be defined as a process of moving, either across an international border, or within a nation. It involves a population on the move, encompassing any kind of movement of people, whatever its length, composition and causes; it includes migration of refugees, displaced persons, uprooted people, and economic migrants. Migration is a global phenomenon that is growing in scope and complexity, affecting most countries, families, communities, and almost every aspect of modern life. An international migrant is defined as "a person who leaves their country of origin, or the country of habitual residence, to establish themselves either permanently or temporarily in another country."[3] Consequently, an international migrant changes his or her place of usual residence and crosses an international border.

As of mid-year 2020, while writing this book, there were about 272 million international migrants in the world. Because the number of international migrants is growing faster than the total population, their share of the world's population has been increasing. Currently, international migrants comprise 3.5 per cent of the global population of 7.5 billion people, compared to 2.8 per cent in the year 2000. Just over half of all international migrants reside in Europe and Northern America. In 2019, Europe hosted the largest number of international migrants (82.3 million), followed by North America (58.6 million) and North Africa and Western Asia (48.6 million).[4]

To make these figures a bit more personal, let's look at a true story. Melissa was five years old when she and her family left Cartagena, Colombia. In the 80s and 90s, Colombia went through a big civil war and so life there was very hard. Her family decided to emigrate to the United States to seek a better life and education. Through a long and costly process, they managed to come to the US and settled in Florida. The experience of living in a new country was scary and confusing for Melissa. She recalled being intimidated and bullied by the other kids during the first days in kindergarten because she was not able to speak English. With determination and hard work, Melissa managed to overcome many obstacles to succeed in life. After high school, she entered college and majored in communication. Her journey was not easy for she had to face tough financial situations and to make lots of sacrifices to earn a college degree. Being bilingual, fluent in Spanish and English, Melissa ended up in Washington, D.C., and worked as a manager of communication for the Washington Nationals, a major league baseball team.[5] Melissa's successful story is not uncommon. There are countless of other successful stories of immigrants who have contributed greatly to their host countries. So migration need not end in disaster.

Hospitality to Strangers – A Moral Obligation

Hospitality to strangers and sojourners is an esteemed virtue in the Bible, and the reward to those who practice it is often great. In offering simple hospitality to the three strangers at odd hours of the day, Abraham was rewarded with a special revelation—namely the news of the birth of the promised son Isaac (Genesis 18:1-10). In the time of famine, the widow of Zarephath hosted a starving stranger who happened to be the prophet Elijah the Tishbite. For her act of kindness, she was rewarded with an unlimited supply of flour and oil (1 Kings 17:1-16). The third example comes from the book of the law where Israel is reminded of her "alienness" and that her blessings depend upon how she treats the foreigner in the land: "You shall not oppress a resident alien; you know the heart of an alien, for you were aliens in the land of Egypt" (Exodus 23:9). Hospitality to an outsider was so important that it was dictated by the law and built into Israel's legal code (Deuteronomy 10:19; Leviticus 24:22). In the New Testament, Jesus is consistently portrayed as a stranger, guest, host, and even as food. Such depictions of Jesus highlight the virtue of hospitality. Jesus teaches that when someone feeds the hungry, gives water to the thirsty, clothes the naked, cares for the sick, and visits the prisoner—in other words, welcomes a stranger— he or she does it for Christ himself (Matthew 25:31-46). The Letter to the Hebrews states, "Do not neglect to show hospitality to strangers, for thereby some have entertained angels unawares" (13:2). In another letter, Peter exhorts his fellow Christians saying, "Practice hospitality ungrudgingly to one another" (1 Peter 4:9). Accordingly, hospitality to the stranger is a major pastoral challenge of migration today. Solidarity with and welcoming the immigrants in our midst is a Christian moral obligation.

Hospitality to the stranger was a highly regarded virtue worldwide in antiquity and by many religions. For the ancient Greeks, hospitable treatment of strangers was a mark of civility and piety. In Greek mythology, the divine frequently took on the appearance of a stranger. In the *Odyssey*, for example, Athena, who is the goddess of victory and wisdom, appears in various disguises to assist Odysseus: as a young maiden carrying a pitcher, as an ordinary man, and as a beautiful skilled woman. For the Romans, hospitality was divinely sanctioned, because receiving a stranger was an obedience to divine will and therefore divine law (technically, *ius Dei*). Some Romans considered hospitality to a guest as even loftier than receiving a friend, for offering to friends comes naturally, but hosting a guest requires more motivation and altruism.

For Asians, hospitality to strangers is considered an important religious virtue. In the Buddhist tradition, for instance, the teaching of *Dana* (generosity or hospitality) is a basic virtue that every Buddhist must practice from the beginning stages of the spiritual life.[6] Without *Dana*, Enlightenment, which is a state of perfect knowledge and bliss, can never be achieved. According to Taoism, which is a Chinese mystical philosophy founded by Lao-tzu in the sixth century BC, to obtain long life and good fortune one must show compassion and practice hospitality to strangers.

In Islam, too, the Prophet Muhammad teaches the importance of hospitality to the stranger. The Qur'an states: "Be kind to parents, and the near kinsman, and to orphans, and to the needy, and to the neighbor who is of kin, and to the neighbor who is a stranger, and to the companion at your side, and to the traveler, and to [slaves] that your right hands own" (*Qur'an* 4.36-37).

The world's great religious traditions, then, have long affirmed the connection between religion and hospitality to strangers. The Judeo-Christian tradition especially highlights this motif, not only as a moral responsibility but as a spiritual practice, a way of life or a *habitus*. Since hospitality is love in action, it is the most appropriate response to the immigration and migration issue today.

There are many ways to practice hospitality. We can begin by being generous with and practicing charity toward our friends and neighbors. But we cannot and must not end there! The religious practice of hospitality must go beyond family, acquaintances, and even fellow citizens. Genuine hospitality reaches out to those we do not yet know, particularly to the immigrants who are in our midst and at our borders. By extending ourselves to these vulnerable ones we might not only entertain angels but actually meet God face to face.

For Reflection:

- What do you think is the significance of Israel's memory of their founding ancestors as resident aliens, strangers, sojourners, or (more appropriately) immigrants?

- Hospitality to strangers was a highly regarded virtue worldwide in the Bible and by many world religions. Why do you think this is so?

- What is the responsibility of a believer and a faith community for addressing the crisis of global migration?

Chapter Two

The Tragedy of Human Trafficking

Human trafficking is a universal problem. It is a scourge that exists across the entire globe. It is a horrific crime that hides in plain sight and causes immense suffering for countless victims who are often the most vulnerable among us. It is also extremely lucrative. This modern-day slave trade is a threat to all nations and triggers all sorts of grave violations of human rights. It shatters families and communities, fuels organized crime, and undermines public health and security.

A Contemporary Global Scourge

The United Nations defines human trafficking as:

> The recruitment, transportation, transfer, harboring or receipt of persons, by means of the threat or use of force or other forms of coercion, of abduction, of fraud, of deception, of the abuse of power or of a position of vulnerability or of the giving or receiving of payments or benefits to achieve the consent of a person having control over another person, for the purpose of exploitation.[7]

Human smuggling, which is a related but different crime, generally involves the consent of the person(s) being smuggled. These people often pay large sums of money to be smuggled across international borders. Once in the country of destination, they are generally left to their own devices. However, smuggling becomes trafficking when the element of force or coercion is introduced.

A Huge Business Syndicate

The three most common types of human trafficking are forced labor, debt bondage, and sex trafficking. Forced labor, also known as involuntary servitude, is the biggest sector of trafficking in the world. For instance, a family gives up a child to an adoption agent in Nepal because they cannot afford to care for him. The child is then, in turn, sold to a sweatshop owner who forces the child to learn to sew garments without pay for hours each day. The child is usually malnourished and does not attend school. This is a typical example of forced labor or involuntary servitude.

Debt bondage is another form of human trafficking in which an individual is forced to work in order to pay a debt. For example, a young woman from Russia has accumulated serious credit card debt and is desperate to pay it off. A man who identifies himself as an employment agent offers her a job in the United States as a domestic worker. She arrives in San Francisco with a valid visa, but her passport is immediately confiscated. She is brought to a home where her movement is restricted. She is then told that she must work as a housekeeper to pay off the cost of her travel or her family will be killed. The young woman is in debt bondage.

The third type is sex trafficking. Two women from Southeast Asia are brought into Los Angeles under the pretense that they will receive jobs as hostesses or waitresses. When they arrive, they are held captive and forced into prostitution, while their captor controls the money they receive. Sex trafficking disproportionately affects women and children and involves forced participation in commercial sex acts. In the United States, any child under the age of eighteen who has been involved in a commercial sex act is considered a trafficking victim. Women and girls make up eighty percent of the people trafficked transnationally. Yearly, traffickers exploit about one million children in the commercial sex trade. For example, a fifteen-year-old boy runs away from his home in San Jose, California and ends up living on the streets of Los Angeles. He is seduced by a pimp who forces him into prostitution and controls all the acquired profits.

Human trafficking is the second largest and fastest growing criminal industry in the world with as many as forty million individuals living in slavery-like conditions.[8] Many mega-cities around the world harbor this illegal activity. Cities like Paris, London, Amsterdam, Tokyo, New York, San Francisco, just to name a few, are not immune to the problem, and have been considered prime destinations for human trafficking due to their ports, airports, industry, and rising immigrant populations. The International Labor Organization (ILO) estimated that in 2017 sex trafficking and labor trafficking generated $99 billion and $51 billion in revenues worldwide, respectively. To put it into perspective, human trafficking almost matches the annual revenue of Starbucks, Nike, Facebook, and Disney combined, approximately $152 billion.

What, if anything, can the Bible possibly say to us about the scandal of human trafficking?[9] I strongly believe that there is an urgent need for all Christians to respond to and become involved in tackling this modern day slavery. Just as the abolitionists responded to the great injustice of the slave trade in the eighteenth and nineteenth centuries, so must we respond to this global scourge and crime of contemporary human trafficking. The Bible actually has a lot to say about this matter.

The Brother Who Was Trafficked

Like so many victims of trafficking today, Joseph was sold by his own family. His story is recounted in the book of Genesis (chapters 37-50). Joseph was the eleventh son of Jacob but Rachel's firstborn. Of all the sons, Joseph was most favored by his father. As such, his brothers were quite jealous of Joseph and plotted to kill him. But when the brothers saw a caravan of merchants heading to Egypt, they decided instead to sell Joseph to these merchants for twenty pieces of silver. The fact that the Midianite caravan was ready to buy a slave to sell in Egypt (Genesis 37:26-28) tells us that the slave trade was already happening in the region at that time.

Joseph was later sold to Potiphar, one of Pharaoh's officials in Egypt. While he was attending to his daily tasks, Potiphar's wife tried to seduce Joseph, who is described as "handsome and good-looking" (Genesis 39:6). Joseph however resisted her sexual advances and ran away. Angered by his refusal, she made a false accusation of rape against Joseph, and he was therefore thrown into prison.

As a slave, Joseph had no rights and no way to appeal when he was unjustly accused by Potiphar's wife. This is similar to the experience of many trafficking victims, who are vulnerable to abuse. They are often falsely accused and are imprisoned for crimes they did not commit. Unfortunately, there are far too many cases of young teenage girls who could not resist and therefore are sexually and physically abused by their employers. Statistically, women and girls are disproportionately affected by modern slavery, accounting for about seventy-one percent of the overall total, while men and boys account for twenty-nine percent.

While in prison, Joseph became famous for interpreting dreams. One day, Pharaoh dreamt of seven lean cows, which devoured seven fat cows, and of seven withered ears of grain that devoured seven fat ears. When Pharaoh's advisers failed to interpret the dream, a fellow prisoner remembered Joseph. Joseph was then summoned. He interpreted the dream as seven years of abundance followed by seven years of famine, and advised the Pharaoh to store up surplus grain. Following the prediction, Joseph was released from prison and appointed as a vizier, a high-ranking official in Egypt.

Just as there are many twists and turns in the story of Joseph, there are also many lessons one can learn. One important lesson is that although Joseph was a vulnerable victim, he was still created in the image of God (Genesis 1:26), and thus, God continued to care for him and protect him. Three times in Joseph's story the phrase, "But God was with him" (Genesis 39:2, 21, 23), is repeated, reminding us that no matter how terribly we are treated by others, whether one is sold, betrayed, falsely accused, unjustly imprisoned, and forgotten, God's presence can carry us through difficult times. Furthermore, we are created equally in the image and likeness of God. That is something no one can take away from us no matter how defenseless we have become. The remarkable thing about Joseph is that, as a trafficking survivor, he did not lose hope and faith. Sustained by God's mercy, Joseph was able to forgive his brothers who had sold him into slavery. Through Joseph, the whole family of Jacob was saved from a famine and was reunited with him in Egypt. Unfortunately, most trafficking survivors do not end so favorably. As Christians, we cannot and must not stand idly by and allow millions to be exploited by the unjust and criminal acts of human trafficking. We all have a moral duty to liberate these vulnerable captives.

Setting the Captives Free

The Torah (Jewish Law) forbade human trafficking of fellow Israelites, and the penalty for those who committed this terrible crime is death. The Book of Deuteronomy states, "If someone is caught kidnapping another Israelite, enslaving or selling the Israelite, then that kidnaper shall die. So you shall purge the evil from your midst" (24:7). This commandment of the Law is very clear and direct. Human trafficking is an abomination and the person who commits this crime must be removed from society.

The biblical prophets were very strong in speaking out against injustices to the poor and the vulnerable. The prophet Joel protests against human trafficking, including the selling of children in exchange for prostitutes and wine, and warns that similar things could happen to their own children (Joel 4:1-3). The prophet Amos strongly objects to the practice of human trafficking, chastising Israel "because they sell the righteous for silver, / and the needy for a pair of sandals" (Amos 2:6-7). Amos later writes, "[L]et justice roll down like waters, / and righteousness like an ever-flowing stream" (Amos 5:24).

The author of the Book of Proverbs admonishes everyone to "Speak out for those who cannot speak, / for the rights of all the destitute. / Speak out, judge righteously, / defend the rights of the poor and needy" (Proverbs 31:8-9). These principles can certainly apply to those hurt and victimized through the illegal practice of human trafficking.

Following the directives of the Law, Prophets, and Wisdom tradition, Jesus worked to liberate those who were held captives. Liberating the oppressed was his primary goal and mission. At his inaugural address at Nazareth, Jesus cited the words of the prophet Isaiah to announce his vocation and mission: "The Spirit of the Lord is upon me, / because he has anointed me to bring good news to the poor. / He has sent me to proclaim / release to the captives and recovery of sight to the blind, / *to let the oppressed go free*, / to proclaim the year of the Lord's favor" (Luke 4:18-19; italics added for emphasis). The reading that Jesus selected is actually a combination of Isaiah 61:1-2 and 58:6. This composite quotation defines Jesus' prophetic mission and ministry, fulfilling Isaiah's prophecy.

Human trafficking is contemporary slavery. It is basically holding someone in bondage and stealing that person's freedom and dignity. It is a vile crime against God and humanity. It treats a human life as if it were only a commodity that can be bought and sold, used and discarded. Consequently, this crime contradicts everything God has formed and fashioned, a human person who is so beautifully created in God's very own image (Genesis 1:26-27; see also Psalm 139:14). It is no wonder that Jesus works so hard to restore the dignity of the human person. Jesus' teaching of the Golden Rule summarizes the entire Torah: "In everything, do to others as you would have them do to you; for this is the law and the prophets" (Matthew 7:12). Jesus repeatedly taught the obligation to love our neighbors (Matthew 19:19) and those who are victimized (Luke 10:25-37).

Emancipation

Slavery was quite normal in the Greco-Roman times, yet many New Testament writers opposed it. While Saint Paul, for example, did not explicitly call for a systematic eradication of slavery, Paul must have questioned the values that perpetuated it. We have one concrete example where the apostle Paul dealt with the issue of slavery. It is found in the letter to Philemon.

Philemon is one of the shortest letters in the New Testament. It is only twenty-five verses long. The letter concerns a run-away slave named Onesimus. Onesimus must have done something terribly wrong. He might have stolen money or something precious that he could not possibly pay back and therefore had to run away from his master Philemon. Philemon was a well-to-do Christian, a slave owner, and a patron of the church at Colossae. Paul seems to know Philemon well for Paul calls him a "beloved friend and fellow worker" (Philemon 1). Paul may have introduced Philemon to the Christian faith and that would explain why Paul reminded Philemon that he owed him "his very self" (verse 19). Sometime after his escape, Onesimus came into contact with Paul. Onesimus may have been arrested and imprisoned alongside Paul. Paul was definitely in prison when he wrote this letter (see verses 1, 9, 13 and 23). After meeting Paul, Onesimus was converted and also became a Christian believer. Paul and Onesimus became very close, like father and son (verse 10). Although Paul preferred to keep Onesimus with him, Paul was obligated to send Onesimus back to Philemon because he was technically Philemon's property, while realizing that he might be severely punished. According to Roman law, the owner of a runaway slave could inflict any kind of punishment that was fitting to the crime, even to the extent of execution. This was a major concern of Paul and the reason for writing to Philemon, asking that he accept Onesimus back "no longer as a slave but as more than a slave, a beloved brother" (verse 16).

What exactly was Paul asking Philemon to do? I believe it was more than just a request for forgiveness and reconciliation between a master and a slave. Paul's appeal was much more radical, namely, to set Onesimus free! The technical term for setting a slave free is called, "manumission." The request that Paul was asking Philemon, the slave owner, who was also his "beloved friend and fellow worker," to do was something out of the ordinary for his time. Did Philemon grant Paul's request to free Onesimus? The preservation of this remarkable letter, which made it into the Christian canon, suggests that Philemon did. Tradition maintains that Onesimus was set free, became a bishop in Ephesus, and was martyred in Rome around 95 AD.

How Paul dealt with the issue of slavery in the letter to Philemon is consistent with what he dealt with in other letters. Paul frequently invited the early Christians to live in a new kind of freedom without distinction that is based on ethnicity, status, and gender. He taught that in Christ "There is no longer Jew or Greek, there is *no longer slave or free*, there is no longer male and female; for all of you are one in Christ Jesus" (Galatians 3:28, italics added for emphasis).

In the letter to Timothy, Paul explicitly condemned "slave traders" for he considered it to be immoral, similar to the crime of murder (1 Timothy 1:9-10). The author of the Book of Revelation also recognized the abhorrence of human trafficking and commanded that Christians should not take part in it (Revelation 18:13). Merchants who trade human beings like other commodities will be dealt harsh punishment and destruction by God (Revelation 18:20).

Human trafficking is a gross offence against men, women, and children who are created in God's image. As Christians, we have an obligation to speak out against this modern-day slavery that people over the centuries had worked so hard to eradicate. In 1863, Abraham Lincoln, the sixteenth President of the United States, issued the Emancipation Proclamation declaring, "that all persons held as slaves are and henceforward shall be free." Two years later, the United States ratified the thirteenth Amendment that officially abolished slavery. Yet, ironically, there are far more people enslaved today than during the transatlantic slave trade of the seventeenth and eighteenth centuries. Slavery is a devastating assault on human dignity. We still have much work to do to eradicate this terrible scourge.

For Reflection:

- From a Christian point of view, what is wrong with slavery? Furthermore, why is it immoral that a person is viewed as a commodity or the property of another?

- Read Paul's little letter to Philemon. If you were Philemon, how would you respond to Paul's request?

Chapter Three

The Plight of Refugees and Asylum Seekers

There are many reasons why people move. Some voluntarily choose to leave their homelands in order to find a better way of life. Others are forced to abandon their homes due to drought, flooding, or deforestation. A larger number of immigrants however leave because of political conflict, religious persecution, or a combination of both. These folks are usually designated as refugees who have been forced to leave their country due to violent conflict. Refugees normally want to return to their homeland once the war is over. However, these situations often lead to years of displacement. Many seek asylum elsewhere because they simply have no recourse whatsoever to return home.

Take for example the story of George, his wife Ani, and their twins. They once had a prosperous lifestyle in the Syrian city of Aleppo, but owing to the war in Syria, they were forced to flee to Armenia. Starting a new life in a foreign country was quite tough. They tried as hard as they could to make ends meet in their new home. But the COVID-19 pandemic in 2020 only made it harder. George's work as a taxi driver dried up and Ani's business of baking bread for neighbors stalled. As a national lockdown took hold, it became even more difficult to pay rent on their apartment. "We have to struggle every day of our life in Armenia relying on the support from others, hoping for a better future for ourselves and our children," said Ani. "We can hardly pay the bills."[10]

Since the Syrian civil war began in 2011, families have suffered under brutal conflict that has killed hundreds of thousands of people, torn the nation apart, and set back the standard of living by decades. After a decade of civil strife, the Syrian war caused the largest refugee and displacement crisis of our time. About 5.6 million Syrians became refugees, and another 6.2 million people were displaced within Syria. Nearly 12 million people in Syria needed humanitarian assistance. At least half of the people affected by the Syrian refugee crisis were children.

As of mid-year 2020, the number of refugees worldwide was estimated at 26 million. We are now witnessing a record high number of refugees and asylum-seekers due to conflict, war, persecution, and human rights violations. Interestingly, the Bible also has much to say about this current global crisis.

Moses and the Israelites as Refugees

To migrate is to move! One of the most powerful experiences of migration in the Bible is the Exodus story. Throughout this second book of the Bible, God is portrayed as a migrant sojourning with the Hebrews. The book portrays two main refugee accounts: first, the story of Moses fleeing from Pharaoh and seeking sanctuary in the land of Midian (Exodus 2:11-22), and second, the story of the Hebrews seeking refuge in the wilderness from the oppressive power of Egypt (Exodus 14-15). Moses' plight and Israel's escape are commonly perceived as stories of refugees and seeking asylum.

The opening verses of Exodus reveal that all the descendants of Jacob, including Joseph who was sold into slavery by his brothers, have now settled in Egypt for a while. They have done well in a foreign land and they have become very numerous. But the situation is quickly changing. An ominous note of oppression and enslavement is about to happen because "a new king, who knew nothing of Joseph, came to power" (Exodus 1:8). The king was afraid of the growth and might of the Israelites. Furthermore, he feared that the Israelites might join forces with his enemies and therefore attack Egypt. The king was rather paranoid. Who could blame him, for a similar case had happened to Egypt about a century earlier when Egypt was ruled by the infamous Hyksos kings (about 1650-1525 BC).

The Hyksos were likely Semites, originally from Canaan and Syria. They had invaded or possibly emigrated during a period when Egypt was politically and economically weak. In time and through population increase, they were able to take over and rule at least the northern part of the Nile Valley. It is believed that the pharaoh Ahmose was the one who finally defeated the Hyksos and drove them out of Egypt around 1525 BC. This could very well be the historical context of Exodus 1, and if it is historically reliable, we can understand the new pharaoh's xenophobia (literally, "fear of foreigners") about the population growth and potential threat of the Israelite people.

To curb the population growth, Pharaoh began to oppress the Israelites by forcing them into hard physical labor. Their primary tasks were to make bricks for Pharaoh's building projects and to do other menial forms of hard work. Like many migrant workers today, the Israelites were performing the 3D jobs: "Dirty, Dangerous, and Demeaning."

Even worse, the Israelites had become Pharaoh's slaves. Yet, the more Pharaoh oppressed them, the more they multiplied and spread (Exodus 1:12). So paranoid was Pharaoh that he ordered newborn Hebrew boys to be killed by the midwives during their deliveries (Exodus 1:15-16). The famous hero who was born in Egypt during this period of oppression and survived the massacre of Pharaoh was none other than Moses. His story has captured the imagination of many artists and has been made into several Hollywood blockbuster movies, for example: *The Ten Commandments* in 1956, the popular Disney animation, *The Prince of Egypt* in 1998, or the more recent box office thriller, *Exodus: Gods and Kings* in 2014. With Christian Bale as Moses, the movie *Exodus* collected hundreds of millions of dollars.

These movies creatively and dramatically portray the oppression of the Israelites and life of the protagonist Moses. They show how the infant Moses was miraculously saved from Pharaoh's genocide and ended up being reared in the royal court. Moses eventually discovered his true identity.

In an intervention to stop an Egyptian taskmaster from beating a Hebrew worker, who happened to be his kinsman, Moses killed the Egyptian. Fearing Pharaoh's retribution, Moses fled Egypt seeking refuge in the land of Midian (Exodus 2:11-15). Midian is a mountainous and desert-like area located on the eastern side of the Sinai Peninsula in the northwestern part of modern Saudi Arabia.

While wandering in the desert, Moses defended some women who were harassed by bandits. The women turned out to be the daughters of Jethro, the priest of Midian. Because of his act of bravery, Moses was welcomed to live with Jethro and work for him. Eventually, Moses married his daughter Zipporah and became a legal "resident alien," usually referred to as a *ger* in Hebrew. As a legal *ger* of the land, Moses ceased to be an unwelcome "foreigner" (a *nekhar* or *zar* in Hebrew). When his wife Zipporah bore a son, Moses named him *Ger-shom*, saying "I am a *legal immigrant* in a foreign land" (Exodus 2:22; emphasis added). By naming his son *Ger* plus *shom* ("foreign land"), Moses was actually acknowledging his status as a legal immigrant or "resident alien." The explanation of his son's name comes up again in Exodus 18:3. In both passages, Moses describes himself as a legal immigrant (*ger*) living in a foreign land (*shom*).

In the midst of this refugee crisis, God called Moses and commissioned him to return to Egypt to confront Pharaoh and liberate the Israelites from Egypt (Exodus 3:4-10). What the Lord said to Moses is quite powerful and touching, especially for those who are immigrants or refugees: "I have observed the misery of my people who are in Egypt; I have heard their cry on account of their taskmasters. Indeed, I know their sufferings" (Exodus 3:7). God not only knows the misery of those who suffer but actually feels their pains and hears their cry for mercy and justice. But Pharaoh's heart was hardened, and so he refused to let God's people go.

The Israelites were permitted to leave only after numerous calamitous plagues, climaxing with the death of the eldest sons of the Egyptians, including Pharaoh's own son. For forty years, the Israelites became landless and refugees wandering about in the desert. Their experience as refugees was harsh and was indelibly impressed in their collective memory (for example, Deuteronomy 26:5-6; Psalm 105:23; Micah 6:4). It is therefore not surprising that laws regarding immigrants figure so prominently in the Torah.

The reason for Israel giving special consideration to the plight of strangers, migrants, and refugees in a foreign land is rooted in Israel's own experience of mistreatment in Egypt. Although the laws regarding immigrants will be treated in detail later in this book, two notable examples are worth mentioning. Along with many other law codes, Israel was commanded to take special care of the sojourners in their midst: "You shall not wrong or oppress a resident alien, for you were aliens in the land of Egypt" (Exodus 22:21), and "You shall not oppress a resident alien; you know the heart of an alien, for you were aliens in the land of Egypt" (Exodus 23:9). So important is this divine directive that it is mentioned twice in Israel's legal document called the Covenant Code (see Exodus 20:23—23:19).

Jesus the Estranged and Displaced Son of God

There is an obvious parallel between the lives of Moses and Jesus, especially in the Gospel of Matthew. Many scholars have noted that Matthew specifically portrays Jesus as the New Moses. The five discourses of Jesus in Matthew correspond with the Five Books of the Torah. But perhaps the most noted parallelism is found in the infancy narrative of chapter two of the Gospel of Matthew.

Right after Jesus' birth, Matthew recounts the dramatic exodus of the Holy Family escaping the wrath of King Herod who felt threatened by the news of the birth of a new king in Bethlehem. The story of Jesus, Joseph and Mary seeking refuge in Egypt obviously reinforces the underlying theme of the Moses-Jesus typology. An informed reader would notice its allusions to Exodus 1-2: a powerful but fearful ruler issued a death decree, a flight to escape the death threat, a slaughter of innocent children, and a return after the wicked ruler is dead.

According to historians, Herod was a wicked ruler who reigned with fear, suspicion, murders, and intrigue. Herod's brutality and paranoiac suspicion of his rivals point to the truth of an ancient joke: "It was better to be Herod's pig than his son." Under such horrific circumstances, migration was the only means of survival, especially when Herod intentionally sought to destroy the infant Jesus.

Withdrawal from opposition is sometimes absolutely necessary. Joseph therefore obeyed an angel's command in a dream, took the child and his mother "by night," and swiftly fled to Egypt for refuge. Consequently, Jesus, Mary, and Joseph became asylum seekers. Without travel documents, they crossed borders looking for safety and sanctuary. Like many other immigrants before and after them, Jesus and his family were political refugees seeking asylum in a country that would open the doors for them. Egypt was the traditional place of refuge for many Israelites in biblical times (1 Kings 11:40; Jeremiah 26:21; Matthew 2:13-15).

It seems that the thrust of the movement of Matthew 2 is to have Jesus as Son of God go into Egypt in order to come out of Egypt, which clearly alludes to Israel's exodus and liberation. Similar to the Israelites in the Old Testament who were sojourners (Abraham and Sarah), immigrants and refugees (Jacob, Joseph, Moses, Jeremiah, Israel in Assyria, and Judah in Babylon), and returnees from exile, Jesus who is the Son of God and Messiah also became a victim of similar experiences—namely, threatened by an evil king, driven into exile, estranged from his own country, and returned to his birthplace in Bethlehem of Judea only to be displaced again to Nazareth in Galilee. Jewish readers would definitely hear Old Testament echoes and allusions in this infancy narrative.

Another literary indication of the Exodus motif is the fulfillment formula in Matthew 2:15 found in Hosea 11:1, "Out of Egypt I have called my son." By quoting Hosea, Matthew provides a scriptural basis for and prophecy-fulfillment of the Messiah's exile and return.

Jesus, who is declared the "Son of God" (Matthew 2:15) in a foreign territory, experienced persecution, alienation, and estrangement like many prophets of old and throughout Israel's salvation history. The child Messiah was displaced and depended upon people's hospitality. He certainly knows what it was really like to be an immigrant and a refugee. Likewise, the adult Jesus who will wander about here and there preaching the Good News (Matthew 9:35) also has no place to lay his head (Matthew 8:20). This Son of God, whose deathbed will be the beams of a cross, yet who will become the Messiah for all, is completely in solidarity with those who are estranged, despised, and ostracized, and promised to be with them until the end of the age (Matthew 28:19-20).

Point of No Return

While Jesus was able to return to Israel his homeland, most refugees do not have that recourse. As noted at the beginning of the chapter, refugees are individuals who typically flee their home country to escape severe religious or political persecution or other factors that violate their human rights. They run away to avoid harm done to them and their family. Thus, they flee to another country to apply for asylum or international protection. Their departure or escape usually means that they have reached a point of no return.

According to the United Nations High Commissioner for Refugees (UNHCR), around one million people seek asylum every year. While everyone has a right to seek asylum from persecution, it is not always possible to determine who qualifies for international protection in order to be granted asylum. During mass movements of refugees, the process becomes more difficult because the requests are too many and the demands too great. These groups of folks who are in a state of "limbo" are often called *prima facie* (meaning "at first sight") refugees. For example, at the end of 2019, there were approximately 4.2 million people around the world waiting for a decision on their asylum claims.[11]

Several modern examples come to mind in Asia and Latin America. Mohammed, a Rohingya refugee who fled to Bangladesh with his family of seven, including a baby born along the way, said with tears streaming down his face, "They burned our house and drove us out by shooting. We walked for three days through the jungle."[12]

Approximately 671,000 Rohingya refugees have fled violence and serious human rights violations in Myanmar since August 2017. Many walked for days through the forest to reach safety in Bangladesh, including pregnant women, young children, the sick, and the elderly. Refugees have spontaneously settled in and around existing refugee communities in two main settlements, Kutupalong and Nayapara, overstretching already-limited services and scarce resources. The Kutupalong refugee settlement has grown to become the largest of its kind in the world, with more than 600,000 people living in an area of just 13 square kilometers, stretching infrastructure and services to their limits.

After decades of conflict and war in Iraq, millions have been forced to abandon their homes. Many continue to flee with just the clothes on their backs and are in desperate need of emergency aid.

Ongoing violence, insecurity, political threats as well as lack of food, medicine, and essential services in Venezuela have compelled countless people, many of whom are women and children, to find shelter and food in neighboring countries. Many arrive scared, tired, and in dire need of basic assistance. This is the largest exodus in the region's recent history. As of mid-2020, there were over 650,000 asylum seekers from Venezuela worldwide.

How Can You Help?

There are many organizations that work around the clock to protect and assist refugees all over the world. One outstanding agency that draws upon a rich tradition of Scripture and Catholic social teaching is Catholic Relief Services (CRS). CRS is known to assist countless refugees and vulnerable migrants around the world. You can check out their website (www.crs.org) to learn about their mission statement and how to get involved.

Another important way is to raise awareness. First, however, one must keep up to date with the latest news and stories of refugees around the globe. One helpful website is the UNHCR we mentioned above (www.unhcr.org). Their latest news releases and stories are tremendously useful.

Another way you can help is to pray regularly for refugees and asylum seekers. The UN has designated June 20 as World Refugee Day every year to honor refugees around the globe. Organizing a day of prayer on June 20 is a very good way to seek strength and courage for people who have been forced to flee their home country to escape conflict or persecution. Celebrating World Refugee Day is an occasion to build empathy and understanding for their plight and to recognize their resilience in rebuilding their lives.

Every action counts. Never underestimate the power of the "mustard seed." Even the smallest gesture of kindness can make an impact. Everyone, no matter how insignificant, has the power to make a difference.

For Reflection:

- In the Bible, God is portrayed as a migrant sojourning with the Israelites in the wilderness. Reflect on the implications of this image of God as one who was always on the move with the people.

- Do you have any collective memory of your family or ancestry as refugees? How does your own experience of migration and asylum help you consider the plight of millions of refugees seeking asylum worldwide?

Chapter Four

Casualties of War and Violence

The most common cause for forced migration around the world is conflict. A recent report reveals that war and violence are the main factors that drive people fleeing to Europe by sea. The report challenges the economic migrant myth, showing that eighty percent of those making perilous sea crossing were forced from their homes due to fear, persecution, and insecurity.

Although forced migration is a global phenomenon, it is more pronounced in Africa. Africa hosts over one-third of the global internal displacement population and it has reached unprecedented levels.[13] At the end of 2018, there were approximately 16.8 million people living in internal displacement as a result of conflict and violence. The Democratic Republic of Congo has the highest number of displaced people on the continent of Africa. Its ongoing conflict and tribal clashes have taken a massive human toll: 4.5 million people are internally displaced (more than any other country in Africa), 7.7 million face acute hunger, 8.5 million are in need of humanitarian assistance, and over six hundred thousand are refugees in surrounding countries. Yet most people have heard almost nothing about it.

When Boko Haram militants stormed into her hometown in Nigeria, Mariam, who was heavily pregnant, dropped everything and ran for her life. Four days after she reached a desert town across the border in neighboring Cameroon, she gave birth in a flimsy tent in a makeshift refugee camp. She wondered how she would care for the baby. "It's so difficult to have a child here. I'm scared," she said.

When the gunfire broke out, elderly resident Frando started to run, and did not look back as neighbors fell around him. "We could hear gunshots behind us," he said shortly after arriving in a refugee camp. "I did not really see what was happening, I only saw corpses lying here and there, people being killed."

Mariam and Frando were among the countless victims and casualties of war and violence. In northeast Nigeria, for example, the Boko Haram insurgency has forced more than 2.5 million people from their homes within the Lake Chad Basin in a desperate search for safety.[14]

What does the Bible say about war and violence and their effects? The Bible recounts many battles and much destruction that inevitably caused many causalities, deportations, and insurmountable sufferings to those who were caught in the crossfire. Three biblical events are worth highlighting.

The Assyrian Captivity

The Jewish Diaspora refers to the dispersion of Jews out of their ancestral homeland of Israel and their settlement in other parts of the globe. There were three major events recorded in the Bible that led the Jews to be dispersed. The first diaspora was orchestrated by the Assyrians.

In the eight century BC, the Assyrian Empire rose to power and threatened the Kingdoms of Israel and Judah. In 722 BC, after a three-year siege, King Sargon II captured Samaria and conquered the northern Kingdom of Israel. Sargon claimed to have carried away over twenty-seven thousand Israelites. This is one of the many instances of forcible relocations implemented by the Assyrian Empire. However, the number was only a tiny fraction of the total casualties. It was likely that many more had already been carried away under previous Assyrian kings, and many more had died in battle or from starvation and disease during the siege. Some historians estimate the number of captives in the hundreds of thousands. The bulk of the population however was not deported but remained behind in their own land or fled south to the Kingdom of Judah.

This event is known as the Assyrian Captivity and is recounted in Second Kings 17:1-15. The author of Second Kings attributed this tragic fall to Israel's kings and the people for "worshiping other gods" (2 Kings 17:7). Interestingly, the prophet Amos had already warned them about the consequences of their idolatry, but they refused to listen to him. Thus, Amos prophesied saying, "Your wife shall become a prostitute in the city, and your sons and your daughters shall fall by the sword, and your land shall be parceled out by line; you yourself shall die in an unclean land, and Israel shall surely go into exile away from its land" (Amos 7:17).

The Babylonian Exile

The second major Jewish dispersion was inflicted by the Babylonians. In the sixth century BC, the might and expansion of the Babylonians threatened the existence of the southern Kingdom of Judah. When King Jehoiakim of Judah refused to pay tribute, King Nebuchadnezzar of Babylon besieged Jerusalem and captured it. He carried away King Jehoiakim and his entire family. The Bible says that Nebuchadnezzar "carried away all Jerusalem, all the officials, all the warriors, ten thousand captives, all the artisans and the smiths; no one remained, except the poorest people of the land" (2 Kings 24:13-14). This first deportation of Jews to Babylon took place in 597 BC. The event is recounted in Second Kings 24:1-17.

It is said that history repeats itself. When King Zedekiah, who succeeded King Jehoiakim, revolted against the king of Babylon by entering into an alliance with the Pharaoh of Egypt and refusing to pay tribute, King Nebuchadnezzar returned with a vengeance, defeated the Egyptians, and again besieged Jerusalem, resulting in the second deportation and the city's complete destruction in 587 BC. Second Kings describes the capture of Zedekiah in dramatic fashion: "Then they captured the king and brought him up to the king of Babylon at Riblah, who passed sentence on him. They slaughtered the sons of Zedekiah before his eyes, then put out the eyes of Zedekiah; they bound him in fetters and took him to Babylon." The entire affair is recounted in Second Kings 25:1-11.

Intriguingly, the prophet Jeremiah had warned and prophesied about Jerusalem's fall, but his warnings were ignored (Jeremiah 34:1-7). He was even branded as an imposter and a traitor. Jeremiah was imprisoned and eventually exiled to Egypt. The accounts of the capture and destruction of Jerusalem are vividly described in Jeremiah 52:1-34.

The Babylonian exile was devastating for the Jews. It is estimated that about twenty-five percent of the population of Judah was taken into Babylon as captives or slaves. The Jerusalem Temple, known as the First Temple, was completely destroyed, and Jerusalem and its walls were leveled to the ground. The words of Psalm 137 really capture the tragic moment of the Jews in captivity:

> By the rivers of Babylon – there we sat down and there we wept when we remembered Zion. / On the willows there we hung up our harps. / For there our captors asked us for songs, / and our tormentors asked for mirth, saying, "Sing us one of the songs of Zion!" / How could we sing the Lord's song in a foreign land? / If I forget you, O Jerusalem, let my right hand wither! / Let my tongue cling to the roof of my mouth, / if I do not remember you, if I do not set Jerusalem above my highest joy. / Remember, O Lord, against the Edomites the day of Jerusalem's fall, / how they said, "Tear it down! Tear it down! Down to its foundations!" / O daughter Babylon, you devastator! / Happy shall they be who pay you back what you have done to

us! / Happy shall they be who take your little ones and dash them against the rock!

The prayers and the cry of the poor were heard (Psalm 34). In 539 BC, the Persian King, Cyrus the Great, defeated the armies of Babylon and permitted the exiled Jews to return to Judah to rebuild Jerusalem and its temple. The return of the exiles was a gradual process rather than a single event. Many of the deportees and their descendants did not return. They settled permanently in the lands of exile, for example Babylon and Egypt, and established communities outside the land of Israel, which became known as the Jewish Diaspora.

While the Babylonian Captivity was a tragic event in Israel's history, the exilic period was quite rich in contributing to the Hebrew Scriptures or the Old Testament. Numerous books of the Bible relate the experience of the exile, including the last sections of Jeremiah, Second Kings, and Second Chronicles. Other works from or about the exile include the opening chapters of Ezra and Daniel. Books that were produced in exile include: Lamentations, Ezekiel, Tobit, and Judith. It is believed that the final redaction or editing of the Pentateuch (the five books of the Torah) took place in exile during the Persian period.

The Fall of Jerusalem in 70 AD

Palestine in the first century AD was ruled by the Romans through local client kings, Roman prefects, or governors.

Jesus, for example, was born in Bethlehem around 4 BC during the reign of the client King Herod the Great and was put to death by the Roman prefect Pontius Pilate. Except for minor clashes and uprisings, there was relative peace in the land. In the mid-60s AD, however, the political situation in Palestine became turbulent and volatile. Burdened with excessive taxation and oppressive domination, the Jews rebelled against Rome for independence. The rebellion, known as the First Jewish Revolt, was successful in the beginning. The rebels killed many Roman soldiers and expelled them from Jerusalem. In response, the Roman emperor Nero sent the veteran general Vespasian who crushed the rebels and pushed the majority of the insurgents inside the walls of Jerusalem. In 70 AD, the Roman general Titus besieged Jerusalem. The Romans encircled the city with a wall to completely cut off supplies to the city and thereby drove the insurgents to starvation. The Romans eventually breached the walls of the city and massacred the rebels and many of the remaining inhabitants. They also destroyed the Temple (known as the Second Temple, built mainly by Herod the Great). The Western Wall, also known as the Wailing Wall in Jerusalem, is the only present trace of that magnificent Temple; it remains a site of prayer and pilgrimage today.

Josephus, a Jewish Roman historian of the time, estimated that 1.1 million non-combatants died in Jerusalem, mainly as a result of the violence and famine. Many of the casualties were observant Jews from the diaspora, such as Babylon and Egypt, who had travelled to Jerusalem to celebrate the yearly Passover but instead got trapped in the chaotic siege. Josephus also says that about ninety-seven thousand people were captured and enslaved. Some of these captives were forced to become gladiators and were killed in the arena. Many others were forced to assist in the building of the Roman Forum and the Coliseum in Rome. The children were sold into servitude.

According to the Gospel of Mark, Jesus had already foretold the destruction of Jerusalem and its Temple. The evangelist Mark relates, "As he came out of the temple, one of his disciples said to him, 'Look, Teacher, what large stones and what large buildings!' Then Jesus asked him, 'Do you see these great buildings? Not one stone will be left here upon another; all will be thrown down'" (Mark 13:2). Jesus' prediction of the destruction of the Temple came true in 70 AD when the Romans ransacked Jerusalem. In the Gospel of Luke when Jesus entered the city, he already knew the fate of Jerusalem and thus wept over it saying, "If you, even you, had only recognized on this day the things that make for peace! But now they are hidden from your eyes. Indeed, the days will come upon you, when your enemies will set up ramparts around you and surround you, and hem you in on every side. They will crush you to the ground, you and your children within you, and they will not leave within you one stone upon another; because you did not recognize the time of your visitation from God." (Luke 19:42-44, see also Luke 21:5-24).

Blessed Are the Peacemakers

The biblical situation is sadly evident also today. Ongoing conflicts and civil strife are affecting many countries and displacing millions of people each year. The Office of the United Nations High Commissioner for Refugees (UNHCR), also known as the UN Refugee Agency, appeals to countries worldwide to do much more to find homes for millions of refugees and others displaced by conflict or persecution. A report in 2020 showed that forced displacement is on the rise and with fewer and fewer of those who flee being able to return home.[15]

The movement of people within a country or State involving the establishment of a new temporary or permanent residence is known as internal migration. Internal migration movements can be temporary or permanent and include those who have been involuntarily displaced from their habitual place of residence, as well as people who decide to move to a new place, such as in the case of rural-urban migration. The former are persons or groups of persons who have been forced to flee or to leave their homes, in particular as a result of or in order to avoid the effects of armed conflict, situations of widespread violence, violations of human rights or natural or human-made disasters, and who have not crossed an internationally recognized State border.

At the end of 2019, some 45.7 million people were internally displaced due to armed conflict, extensive violence or human rights violations, according to the Internal Displacement Monitoring Centre (IDMC).[16] Over forty percent of the internally displaced persons (IDPs) occur in three countries: Colombia (7.9 million), Syria (6.1 million), and the Democratic Republic of the Congo (4.5 million).

In the continent of Africa, for instance, internal displacement poses a critical challenge. Africa has consistently been the region most affected by displacement associated with tribal wars over the past decades. Communal violence is a major trigger of displacement. South Sudan's civil war, for example, has uprooted millions of people from their homes since 2013, and hundreds of thousands have been killed. Several ceasefires and peace deals have been signed, none of which held for more than a few months. Addressing the problem requires comprehensive sustainable development strategies and coordinated humanitarian responses. For sure, more peacebuilding efforts are needed across the continent of Africa and many other parts of the world to reduce the crisis of internal displacement.

Every day people suffer and lives are destroyed because of war. But it doesn't have to be this way. One way to respond to this challenge is becoming a peacemaker. The UN defines peacebuilding as follows:

> Peacebuilding aims to reduce the risk of lapsing or relapsing into conflict by strengthening national capacities at all levels for conflict management, and to lay the foundation for sustainable peace and development. It is a complex, long-term process of creating the necessary conditions for sustainable peace. Peacebuilding measures address

core issues that effect the functioning of society and the State, and seek to enhance the capacity of the State to effectively and legitimately carry out its core functions.[17]

Jesus is often called the "Prince of Peace" (Isaiah 9:6-7; see also Luke 2:14; Colossians 1:20) who is truly the embodiment of peacemaking. Jesus' teaching about peacemaking begins with the famous beatitude: "Blessed are the peacemakers, for they will be called children of God" (Matthew 5:9). Peacemakers foster mediation, which helps resolve conflict. Most of the time mediation happens informally between friends, family members, neighbors, schoolmates, and business associates. These blessed peacemakers are called "children of God." According to Jesus, peacemaking is an urgent priority that even transcends worship. Jesus said, "When you are offering your gift at the altar, if you remember that your brother or sister has something against you, leave your gift there before the altar and go; first be reconciled to your brother or sister, and then come and offer your gift" (Matthew 5:23-24).

Jesus' teaching about peace and peacemaking best equips the church to be hospitable and attain durable solutions in a multi-ethnic and multi-religious world. Hence, peacebuilding efforts in our community and world should be encouraged and supported. This is something with which we can all get involved. One can join different networks to become a peacebuilder and bridge builder in his/her own community. One can also join an online platform to host discussions, exchanges or conversations from anywhere around the world to promote interculturality, respectful dialogue, and harmony. Another possible way is to donate on a regular basis to support peacebuilding efforts in the most fragile conflict zones.

For Reflection:

- Why does the Bible recount so many scenes of war and destruction? What do you think is the primary lesson of the Jewish captivities and dispersions recounted in the Bible?

- Discuss Jesus' famous beatitude, "Blessed are the peacemakers, for they will be called children of God" (Matthew 5:9), in the context of human displacement. Is this teaching a practical and durable solution in volatile situations?

- The prophet Isaiah envisioned a time when there would be true peace saying, "They shall beat their swords into plowshares, / and their spears into pruning hooks; / nation shall not lift up sword against nation, / neither shall they learn war any more" (Isaiah 2:4). Do you think that this vision is ever possible? Why and why not?

Chapter Five

The Perils of Climate Change and Natural Disasters

I could never forget what happened in August 2005. I was teaching and directing a study tour in the Holy Land—Israel/Palestine. On a weekly phone-call to check in on my elderly mother, I was told that hurricane Katrina was heading straight to New Orleans. After a short conversation, we said our goodbyes. For many days after, I was not able to contact my mother to find out what had happened to her. For various reasons, my 85-year-old mother, who lived by herself, did not evacuate with my siblings. I later discovered that she had weathered the raging storms and destructive winds of Katrina. But worse was what happened after the storm. The dam broke and water from the Gulf of Mexico came rushing in to inundate much of the city.

By the grace of God, my mother was rescued from her home by some neighbors and brought to higher ground in a flimsy fishing boat. She was later taken to the Superdome, the infamous evacuation shelter in New Orleans. By this time the city had become lawless and violently dangerous. She was then flown to Austin and then picked up by my siblings in Houston. After ten days of being lost and shipped around, she was completely exhausted and had grown beyond weary. This was the third time in her life that she had lost everything. According to my mother, the disaster of hurricane Katrina was almost as devastating as her two previous displacements, namely, the escapes from the war in North Viet Nam in 1955 and from the Communist invasion of South Viet Nam in 1975. Thankfully, my mother survived Katrina and eventually returned to New Orleans to rebuild. She turned one hundred in 2020.

The Threats of the Environment

When asked why people migrated, the common responses are: better jobs, educational opportunities, family reunification, or fleeing violence and persecution. We rarely hear the threat of climate change in their answer. Nevertheless, the environment and natural disasters, such as hurricanes, floods, famines, or earthquakes are major factors in human mobility. An expert at the UNHCR gives this stern warning, "The earth's climate is changing at a rate that has exceeded most scientific forecasts. Some families and communities have already started to suffer from disasters and the consequences of climate change, forced to leave their homes in search of a new beginning."[18]

According to the Internal Displacement Monitoring Centre (IDMC), in 2019 nearly 2,000 disasters triggered 24.9 million new internal displacements across 140 countries and territories.[19] This figure is said to be three times the number of displacements caused by conflict and violence. Most of the displacements were the result of tropical storms and monsoon rains in South Asia, East Asia, and the Pacific. Four countries accounted for more than 17 million new internal displacements due to disaster: India (5 million), the Philippines (4.1 million), Bangladesh (4.1 million), and China (4 million).

Noah and His Ark – A Terrible Biblical Deluge

Human mobility caused by natural disasters happens quite frequently in the Bible. The most well known biblical story is Noah and his ark found in the Book of Genesis (6:5—9:29). Most children are familiar with this catastrophic deluge. Noah is said to be a righteous man who followed God's commandments. Other inhabitants of earth, however, were corrupt and evil, so much so that God regretted having created them (Genesis 6:11-13). Thus, God decided to wipe out the entire earth with a great flood and start anew. God instructed Noah to build an ark in which he, his sons, and their wives, together with one pair of every male and female of all living creatures, would be saved from the waters of the flood.

Many cultures have myths that involve a flood to explain their origins. Archeologists have discovered tablets bearing flood stories from the Semitic peoples who lived in Mesopotamia, between the Tigris and Euphrates rivers (mostly modern-day Iraq). Two of the tablets are the Sumerian "Gilgamesh Epic" and the Babylonian "Atrahasis Epic." Some scholars believe that the author of Genesis was familiar with the myth of Gilgamesh and possibly adapted it for the Bible's flood story. Others argue that they were independent stories derived from a common language of cultural and mythological metaphors and images.

Another explanation might be closer to the truth. The last major Ice Age ended about 10,000 years ago causing the water levels to rise considerably. Entire seaside communities were destroyed. Some scientists claim that the rising water of the Mediterranean Sea breached a blockage in the Bosporus and flooded a valley that became the Black Sea. This event, known as the Black Sea deluge, would have happened around 5600 BC. Other scientists speculate the cause to be a tsunami or a comet. Perhaps the memory of one or more of these great floods was carried over or transported into the biblical flood story.

More importantly, what is the theological point of the famous biblical deluge? We are told explicitly in Genesis 6:5 that the cause for this tragic flood was human wickedness. Human rebellion, which began in the Garden of Eden (Genesis 3:1-7), had escalated to an intolerable level. Humans had departed from their duties to be image-bearers of God and caretakers of God's creation. So, God needed to begin afresh. Noah, who is blameless and righteous (Genesis 6:9), represents a new creation, or a new "Adam." Thus, the flood story is really about how to make things right again to avoid another flood of biblical proportions. One would hope that the new humanity after Noah would learn from past mistakes and get it right. But time is running out, especially with the crisis of climate change due to global warming.

Droughts and Famines of Biblical Proportions

Too much water can cause floods. Not enough water leads to drought. Global climate change is affecting our earthly home in more ways than ever. Extreme weather conditions like severe heat and excessive dryness of the land have caused frequent droughts leading to extreme shortages of food in many parts of the globe.[20] In several African countries, for example Somalia, Kenya, and Ethiopia, droughts have become increasingly severe, leaving millions of farmers without the ability to grow food. A persistent drought recently left nearly 23 million people across East Africa without enough food to eat. In South Sudan almost half of its population—about 4.9 million people—are going hungry. Without any alternatives, families affected by food shortages are forced to migrate. Often one parent, usually the father, has to abandon his home in the countryside to go to the city to find work to feed his entire family.

There is a global hunger crisis today. In mid-2020, a report from CNN said that the world is facing multiple famines of "biblical proportions."[21] The director of the World Food Programme (WFP) starkly identified ten countries already having more than one million people on the verge of starvation. With the 2020 coronavirus pandemic and its effects, there will be an additional 130 million people pushed to the brink of starvation. When added to the 821 million people already chronically hungry, about one billion people will be in dire situations.[22]

The Bible recounts many famines, too. The first one happened in the time of Abraham and Sarah. Soon after they had just arrived in Canaan, a severe famine broke out forcing them to flee "to Egypt to reside there as an alien, for the famine was severe in the land" (Genesis 12:10). Another famine occurred in the days of Isaac. Instead of going down to Egypt as his father Abraham had done, Isaac was advised by God to seek sustenance among the Philistines in Gerar (Genesis 26:1-2). Perhaps the most devastating famine of all was the one that occurred in Egypt in the days of Joseph. The famine lasted for seven years. Through Joseph's correct interpretation of Pharaoh's dream, he wisely stored up surpluses to prepare Egypt in advance and saved numerous lives from starvation, including the entire clan of Israel (Genesis 41-47; see chapter above).

In the days when judges ruled Israel, there was also a famine that caused Naomi and her family to leave Israel to go to Moab, a foreign and hostile territory. After the death of her husband and two sons, Naomi decided to return home to Bethlehem because there was now food there. Naomi's flight as a migrant was filled with endless grief. She returned home empty-handed except for a foreign Moabite daughter-in-law called Ruth, who insisted on accompanying her mother-in-law to the end saying: "Do not press me to leave you or to turn back from following you! Where you go, I will go; where you lodge, I will lodge; your people shall be my people, and your God my God" (Ruth 1:16).

The Moabite woman turned out to be a blessing in disguise for both Naomi and the lineage of the House of David. The memory of her contribution is preserved in the book bearing her name: Ruth.

During the reign of King David, there were three consecutive years of famine because Saul and his family had wrongly slain the Gibeonites in violation of Israelite's covenant with them (2 Samuel 21:1-14). Years later, Israel was struck with another three years of pestilence and famine. This time it killed 70,000 people. The cause of this is said to be David's sin of taking a census against God's command (1 Chronicles 21:1-15).

In the days of the prophet Elijah, there was a drought that caused a hunger crisis (1 Kings 17:1-16). A poor widow of Zarephath, who generously gave the prophet her last portion of food, survived the famine because her jar of flour and oil never go empty. Another severe famine took place in the days of Elisha that lasted seven years (2 Kings 8:1).

An Extraordinary Famine Relief

The Acts of the Apostles recounts many fascinating events in the life of the early Church. There is one incident that most Christians do not know or often overlook. At Antioch, a certain Agabus prophesied that a severe famine would happen over the entire Roman world. Agabus didn't say exactly when the famine would occur, but Luke, writing many years after the event, inserted an aside note saying that, "this took place during the reign of Claudius" (Acts 11:28). Emperor Claudius ruled from 41-54 AD.

A number of ancient historians mention various crop failures and famines during Claudius' reign. Suetonius (a Roman historian) speaks of a series of droughts causing a scarcity of grain that affected Rome severely (*Claudius* 18.2). Josephus mentions a severe famine that hit Judea around 45-46 AD (*Antiquities* 20:49-53).

To demonstrate their solidarity, the disciples at Antioch organized a relief fund for the poor brothers and the mother-church in Jerusalem. Their action was swift and without hesitation. Luke writes, "The disciples determined that according to their ability, each would send relief to the believers living in Judea" (Acts 11:29). The community chose Barnabas and Paul to deliver the collected relief donation. Although the Church was still at its infant stage, it acted with extraordinary generosity and solidarity.

A Planet in Crisis

The issue of climate change is highly politicized and controversial. But scientific evidence points to it as a reality. The human impact on the environment is a major concern of the twenty-first century. Throughout human history, migration and climate have always been connected, but in the modern era, the impact that humans have made on the environment is likely to force more people to resettle or migrate. Many natural disasters like droughts, hurricanes, floods, or earthquakes are more recurrent and attributed to the effects of climate change, which are now considered to be the key factor of forced migration.

In 2010, a 7.0-magnitude earthquake hit the capital city of Port-au-Prince, leaving 1.5 million Haitians homeless. In 2015, a devastating series of earthquakes hit Afghanistan, Pakistan, and India (7.5-magnitude) and Nepal (7.8-magnitude). These drove hundreds of thousands of residents from their homes. According to a report published in 2017 by Cornell University,[23] events prompted by climate change, such as drought and flooding, could account for up to 1.4 billion people who are forced to migrate by the year 2060. The report also predicts that by the year 2100, two billion people, about one-fifth of the world's population, could become climate refugees due to rising ocean levels.

These alarming predictions should be a wakeup call for all of us to address the global climate change crisis today and to do something about it. We all must act immediately because the planet—our only home—is in great danger. Pope Francis has acknowledged this in one of his major teachings.

Laudato Si'

Latin for "Praised Be to You!," *Laudato Si'* (LS) is the name of Pope Francis' encyclical letter on caring for our common home—planet earth. An encyclical is an official teaching document by the Holy Father. *Laudato Si'* is Pope Francis' second encyclical, published in 2015.[24] In it, the Pope critiqued various human-made factors and symptoms that have caused environmental degradation and global warming. He called all people of the world to take swift and unified action to save mother earth. Humanity is facing an urgent crisis. Because of our actions and carelessness, our planet has begun to look more and more like, in Pope Francis' vivid language, "an immense pile of fifth" (LS, number 21).

The Pope sought to awaken our hearts to move us towards an "ecological conversion" (LS, number 217). A change of heart requires that we renew our relationships with God, one another, and the created world. We are all connected. God created the world and entrusted it to us as a gift. Now, we have the responsibility to care for and protect it and all the people dwelling in it. Protecting human dignity, particularly the poor who are most impacted by climate change and environmental disasters, is strongly linked to care for creation.

Laudato Si' is also a call to action. The Pope appealed to everyone to reject consumerism and resist a capitalist market that does not foster integral human development and social inclusion (LS, number 109). Changes to lifestyle and habits of consumption can make a big difference. For example, we are encouraged to have a re-usable water bottle, take shorter showers, walk, bike, or take public transportation instead of driving, recycle, use compost food waste, and buy energy-efficient appliances. These are just a few concrete examples of how we can respond to the urgency of the present ecological crisis.

This remarkable and revolutionary encyclical of Pope Francis concludes with two prayers. Allow me to cite the first one, "A Prayer for Our Earth," which the Pope encouraged all people to pray:

All-powerful God, / you are present in the whole universe and in the smallest of your creatures. / You embrace with your tenderness all that exits. / Pour out upon us the power of your love, / that we may protect life and beauty. / Fill us with peace, / that we may live as brothers and sisters, harming no one. / O God of the poor, / help us to rescue the abandoned and forgotten of this earth, / so precious in your eyes. / Bring healing to our lives, / that we may protect the world and not prey on it, / that we may sow beauty, not pollution and destruction. / Touch the hearts of those who look only for gain / at the expense of the poor and the earth. / Teach us to discover the worth of each thing, / to be filled with awe and contemplation, / to recognize that we are profoundly united with every creature / as we journey towards your infinite light. / We thank you for being with us each day. / Encourage us, we pray, in our struggle / for justice, love and peace.

For Reflection:

- We are all connected. When we fail to care for creation, what impact does this have on our relationship with ourselves, others, God, and the earth?

- The story of Noah and the Ark in the Book of Genesis is about how to make things right again to avoid another catastrophic flood. In what concrete ways can you slow the rate of global warming and avoid repeating another disaster of biblical proportions?

Chapter Six

Strangers in a Strange Land: The Quest for Home

To be a stranger is to inherently dwell at the margin. As a Vietnamese-American, I live between two cultures. I am neither fully Vietnamese nor fully American; rather, I belong to *both* Vietnamese *and* American cultures. Since I am an immigrant or a "resident alien" as I have been often improperly labeled, I automatically dwell at the margin, a state of being "betwixt and between" two worlds. However, belonging to both cultures and worlds is not all negative. Being "in-between" or at the margin allows me to also be "in-both-and" rather than exclusively one or the other. This experience of liminality enables me to perceive and interpret realities differently. Being a hyphenated person—Vietnamese-American—gives me a new sense of belonging.

Belongingness is the human emotional need to be an accepted member of a group. Whether it is family, friends, co-workers, a religion, a club, or something else, people tend to have a natural desire to belong. Belongingness is a fundamental human motivation and desire, so universal that it is found across all cultures and peoples. We all yearn to go home where we belong.

Longing to Return Home

While being captives in Babylon, the Israelites grieved bitterly of their lonely experience and longed for their homeland. In Psalm 137, the exiles stopped singing and even hung up their "harps," which were instruments of praise, because their sorrow was so deep (see chapter four). The prophet Ezekiel, who was exiled in Babylon, reproached a lot about Israel's past sins, but he also spoke about restoration and a homecoming. God promised those in captivity saying, "I will take you from the nations, and gather you from all the countries, and bring you into your own land" (Ezekiel 36:24; see also 34:12; 37:21). Other prophets too spoke about Israel's deliverance and return (Jeremiah 31:1-22; 33:1-18; Zechariah 10:6-10).

The quest for a home is innate and manifested in every age and culture. It was particularly evident with the first generations of Christian disciples. Their profession of faith in Jesus as the Jewish Messiah caused estrangement and marginalization from the Jewish community and even persecution by many Gentiles who were simply unsympathetic to the Christian movement. The impact of religious hostility and social exclusion forced the early Christians to turn inward for support, strength, and cohesion. The yearning to belong was very important for the early Christians. The question is: What kind of home was the earliest generation of believers longing for and why?[25]

Jesus the Displaced and Homeless One

Mark's Gospel is believed to be the first Gospel to have been composed, likely in Rome around 70 AD. The clues from Mark 13 reveal that this Gospel was written during or soon after the first Jewish war with Rome, which began in 66 AD and reached its climax in the destruction of Jerusalem and its temple in 70 AD (see chapter four). The results of this war and its devastation caused a massive blow to the Jewish people and created a huge crisis of migration called the "Jewish Diaspora." Many Jews were forced to abandon their homes in Jerusalem and escape to the surrounding regions of Palestine and beyond. A large population was taken to Rome as prisoners to be slaughtered in the Coliseum for entertainment or to be sold as slaves. Evidently, Christians were also affected by the rebellion even though they were probably not involved. While many Christians might have fled before the actual war broke out, those who remained in Jerusalem at this time likely emigrated all over the Roman Empire. Literary and archeological evidence show that by the beginning of the second century, there were Christians present in most major cities of the Roman Empire, for example, Antioch, Damascus, Edessa, Ephesus, Philippi, Corinth, Athens, Alexandria, and Rome, just to name a few.

It is within the social and political circumstances of migration and displacement that the evangelist Mark portrays Jesus as a suffering Christ who was the Son of God. Yet he was misunderstood by the people and even by his own disciples, rejected and persecuted by the religious leaders of the time, and left to die alone on the cross. Mark's portrayal of Jesus as the *crucified Christ and abandoned Son of God* purposely provided meaning and encouragement for a community, which was being persecuted for its beliefs and displaced from home. For this evangelist, discipleship literally means picking up one's cross, doing just as their teacher had done (Mark 8:34).

Mark's Gospel begins with a christological confession of Jesus as the Christ who is the Son of God (Mark 1:1; see also 1:11; 9:7; 15:39) with whom his audience can relate and identify. This Jewish Messiah does not come from a royal lineage. His origins are completely unknown. He does not even have a place he calls home. He simply appears in the desert or wilderness (Mark 1:3, 4, 12) where John the Baptist dwelled. The wilderness or desert is considered a place of solitude and temptation. It is often described as the inhospitable dwelling of evil and wild beasts. For Mark's audience the opening scenes of Jesus being in the wilderness (1:2-13) echo the period of Israel's wandering in the desert. Furthermore, the wilderness imagery is symbolic of Jesus' homelessness. Throughout his life and ministry, Jesus moves about as an itinerant preacher who never settled in one place. Just as the opening scenes of the wilderness depict a powerful representation of homelessness, so the Gospel's final scenes of Jesus being crucified and buried in the tomb of a stranger serve as a reminder of Jesus' ultimate experience of homelessness. Jesus' cry on the cross, "My God, my God, why have you forsaken me?" (Mark 15:34) is actually a plea to God for a home.

Jesus as a Guest and Companion

The theme of migration and displacement is also found in the Gospel of Luke. The birth of Jesus is situated at the time when Joseph and Mary had to return from Nazareth to their ancestral home—namely Bethlehem—to enroll in a census imposed by the Emperor Augustus (Luke 2:1-7). In this Gospel, Jesus the divine savior is literally born on the road, sheltered in a stable, and surrounded by animals and shepherds from the field. Likewise, Jesus' entire adult life is portrayed as an itinerant who is often viewed by others as an outsider and a vagabond. Jesus leaves behind family and possessions and calls his followers to do the same (Luke 9:1-6; 10:1-12). He constantly moves about from one town to another without even a place to lay his head: "Foxes have holes, and the birds of the air have nests; but the Son of Man has nowhere to lay his head" (9:58).

Much of Jesus' ministry unfolds while on a journey (Luke 9:51—19:28). Along the way, Jesus is uniquely portrayed as a guest who relied on others for hospitality. Jesus frequently is hosted at meals (5:29; 7:36; 14:1; 22:14; 24:30), and he gets criticized for eating too much (7:34; 5:33) and for socializing with the wrong people (for example, tax collectors and sinners, 5:30; 15:1-2). Consider these scenes. Having been cured of her fever, Simon's mother-in-law "got up immediately and waited on them" (4:39). After responding to Jesus' call to follow him, "Levi gave a great banquet for him in his house" (5:29). Along the journey, Jesus stopped at the home of

Mary and Martha and received hospitality there (10:38-42). He was a guest at the homes of the Pharisees and lawyers (11:37-52; 14:1-24). Having met Jesus, Zacchaeus the tax collector not only invited Jesus into his house and offered him hospitality but promised to give half of his possessions to the poor and repay four times over anyone from whom he had extorted money (19:8). Finally, Jesus dies as a crucified criminal, hanging between heaven and earth and is buried alone outside the city wall in a stranger's tomb. Thus, the evangelist Luke correctly calls him a *paroikos*, which can be translated as a "visitor" (NAB) or "stranger" (NRSV). In the Emmaus story, when asked what they were discussing along the way, the two despairing disciples respond to Jesus, "Are you the only stranger (*paroikos*) in Jerusalem who does not know the things that have taken place there in these days?" (24:18). Evidently, in multiple places the evangelist Luke depicts Jesus as a *paroikos*, which is equivalent to the Old Testament concept of *ger* (singular) or *gerim* (plural) that we noted can be translated in different ways in English: stranger, resident alien, sojourner, or immigrant.

Jesus as Logos Born from Above

It is not surprising for Jesus to feel like a stranger in this world. This view is artfully developed in the Gospel of John. Jesus is portrayed like a temporary resident alien who is constantly crossing borders. He is the divine Word (*Logos* in Greek) who became flesh and dwelt (or literally "pitched his tent") among us (John 1:14); yet the world does not know or accept him. Not surprisingly, Jesus often says in the Gospel of John that his home is not of this world (18:36) but from above (19:11), and therefore he will return to his Father in heaven (16:28).

The motif of Jesus being born from above and thus being estranged is recurrent in John (1:17; 3:17, 31). The emphasis on Jesus as one alienated from this world arises out of the situation in which the Gospel of John was written. The Christians of this community were being or had been expelled from the synagogue (9:22; 12:42; 16:2). The synagogue was much more important than just a place of worship. It was the community center where friends and family members gathered. To be excluded from such a place, especially when they were already estranged from their homeland, would be a devastating shock that caused religious dislocation, social isolation, and psychological trauma.

The community that produced this Gospel (around 90-100 AD) was in deep crisis because they had lost the home where they had worshipped. Why did this happen? The story of the healing of the man born blind in John 9 gives us clues to the historical reconstruction of the separation of the Jewish-Christians from the non-Christian Jews in John's community. In the beginning, both Jews and Christians worshipped side-by-side in the same synagogue. Gradually however the Jewish Christians elevated Jesus above the status of a prophet and even above the position of the Messiah. Eventually they regarded Jesus as the divine and preexistent *Logos* having the same status and nature as God. This christological profession was considered blasphemous and heretical. Such a claim obviously threatened the essence of Judaism. This led to outright hostility and resentment between the Christian Jews and the non-Christian Jews. Thus, the Christian Jews were cast out of the synagogue (see John 9:22; 12:42; 16:2).

Not only were these Christians thrown out of the synagogue, but there appears to have been further persecution such as beatings and imprisonment. As a result of the expulsion and persecution, the Christian group became a small and isolated minority. They became fearful and suspicious of outsiders and hostile toward non-Christian Jews. Consequently, the community turned inward upon itself for support and survival, becoming what scholars classify as a "sect." In a sectarian tone the author records these words of Jesus: "If the world hates you, be aware that it hated me before it hated you. If you belonged to the world, the world would love you as its own. Because you do not belong to the world, but I have chosen you out of the world—therefore the world hates you" (John 15:18-19).

Longing for a Heavenly Homeland

The theme of Christians being strangers and sojourners in the world is also found throughout the New Testament epistles. The author of First Peter, for example, addresses his audience as follows: "To the exiles of the Dispersion in Pontus, Galatia, Cappadocia, Asia, and Bithynia" (1 Peter

1:1). The author identifies the churches located in the five Roman provinces in Asia Minor (modern-day Turkey). It is likely that the "Dispersion" refers to all Christians (Gentile or Jewish) residing in these regions. Several references in the letter (1:1-2; 5:9) indicate that Christianity was widespread in Asia Minor when the letter was written, probably around the turn of the second century (90-110 AD). The social tensions and the suffering reflected in the letter indicate that Jewish and Gentile Christians were despised because their beliefs and values conflicted with those of the society around them. Christians were often misunderstood and even alienated by their neighbors, former friends, and families. Understandably, the author calls these estranged Christians "resident aliens" (*paroikoi*) and "visiting strangers" (*parepidemoi*). These two important Greek terms found in First Peter (1:1, 17; 2:11) are essentially sociological categories that reveal the Christians' self-understanding at this time. The early Christians saw themselves as strangers and sojourners who were seeking a home (Greek *oikos*), in fact, a heavenly one.

The theme of Christians seeking a heavenly homeland is more developed in the letter to the Hebrews. The audience of the letter appears to be suffering from severe social ostracism (Hebrews 10:32-34). The community was forced to redefine itself. The author of Hebrews cleverly depicts Israel's ancestors as "strangers and foreigners" who were seeking a homeland (11:13). But the homeland that they were looking for was not the one that they had departed. The author writes, "If they had been thinking of the land that they had left behind, they would have had opportunity to return.

But as it is, they desire a better country, that is, a heavenly one. Therefore God is not ashamed to be called their God; indeed, he has prepared a city for them" (11:15-16).

In the letter to the Ephesians, the author reminds the Gentile Christians that they were once "strangers" (Greek *zenoi*) because they were without Christ (2:12). Having been redeemed through the blood of Christ, they are no longer "strangers" (*zenoi*) and "aliens" (*paroikoi*) but are "citizens with the saints and also members of the household of God" (2:19). Ephesians, which was probably not written by Paul, appears to be a circular letter intended for many churches residing in Asia Minor around the end of the first century AD. The author points out to his Gentile Christians that although their legal status in the secular and political society has not changed, their theological status has, because of the new relationship with God and the Church. Since they were established upon the foundation of the apostles and prophets, with Christ Jesus as the cornerstone, the author reminds them, "In him the whole structure is joined together and grows into a holy temple in the Lord; in whom you also are built together spiritually into a dwelling place for God" (Ephesians 2:21).

The Church as a Home for All

The Catholic Church recognizes that today's migration makes up the greatest movement of people of all times. This phenomenon has become an increasingly complex problem from social, cultural, political, religious, economic, and pastoral points of view. International migration in particular, or human mobility in general, is a structural component of present-day society's realities. How should the Church respond to this dramatic and troubled sign of the times?

The perfect Christian response is simply *caritas* or "love," which is the essential message of the Church's document called, *Erga Migrantes Caritas Christi* ("The Love of Christ Towards Migrants," EMCC).[26] This Vatican document was published in 2004 by the Pontifical Council for the Pastoral Care of Migrants and Itinerant People to address the migration crisis in the world and to urge all Christians to attend to the pastoral care *for*, *among*, and *with* migrants in the Church. This remarkable document, which remains unknown to most Catholics, invites all Catholics to establish a "culture of welcome" in its communities, without prejudices and biases and without making any distinction among the migrants because of nationality, color, or creed. The document states that the Church is called "to be a fraternal and peaceful meeting place, *a home for all*, a building sustained by the four pillars . . . namely truth and justice, love and freedom." (EMCC, number 100; emphasis added). Furthermore, the document reminds us, "We are all pilgrims on our way towards our true homeland" (EMCC, number 101).

For Reflection:

- How do the Gospels' portrayal of Jesus as the crucified Christ and abandoned Son of God provide meaning and encouragement for those who are being persecuted for their beliefs and displaced from home?

- Where do you feel most at home and experience a sense of belonging? Are you there yet or still looking for it?

Chapter Seven

The Harrowing Ordeals
of Women and Children

The following stories should cause our stomachs to churn. Jazell, who was only 11 years old, was forced to live with a forty-year-old man. She cooked, cleaned, and was forced to have sex. Jazell became pregnant at fourteen and had a baby. The alarming thing is that her father approved of it, and the villagers were silent about it. Another young girl named Rosita who was twelve years old was the target of the sexual desires of a forty-five-year-old man. He paid a small dowry to her parents and received a piece of paper to confirm that it was a valid marriage arrangement. Rosita was raped during the act of the so-called marriage consummation. She got pregnant and had a baby at the age of fourteen.[27] Cham is a nineteen-year-old girl from rural Cambodia. One day a broker arrived to her village promising her a very good paying factory job in China. After obtaining enough money, she said good-bye to her family and set out on a new adventure. She expected to make good money to send back to her family. Her dreams were shattered when she arrived. Cham was forced to marry an older man who repeatedly abused her, both physically and sexually. With all her documents confiscated, she was trapped as an indentured servant.

According to UNICEF, there are more than 700 million women alive who were married before their eighteenth birthday. More than one in three, or about 250 million, had entered into marriage union or became a "child bride" before age fifteen, like Jazell and Rosita.[28] According to one estimate, 14.2 million girls annually, or 39,000 daily, will marry too young.[29] In several countries, taking a child bride has become a cover for pedophilia to avoid the penalties of the law. "Foreign brides," like the case of Cham, who come from Southeast Asian countries of Cambodia, Viet Nam, Indonesia, Thailand, and the Philippines, have been sought after especially by men from Taiwan, Japan, China, and South Korea. Their numbers could run into the hundreds of thousands. In general, feminization of migration in Asia and across the globe has increased significantly in recent years, and the child bride phenomenon is part of this trend.

Female Migrants—A Rising Trend

Women are on the move, more so now than ever before. Women comprise a little less than half, about 47.9 percent or 130 million, of the global international migrant stock (UN DESA, 2019).[30] In comparison to male migrants, female migrants are more vulnerable to mistreatment and usually experience a double discrimination for being women and migrants. Migrant female workers, especially undocumented ones, often suffer extensive violations of human and labor rights. Without papers or legal protection, they are frequently confined in private households. They work long-hours for low wages and their work can be degrading. They are particularly vulnerable to human trafficking, sexual abuse, and prostitution rings. What on earth could the Bible say or teach about these disturbing ordeals of women today?

Strong Migrant Women of the Bible

Biblical authors were well aware of the vulnerability of women in general and widows in particular. The Book of Exodus, for instance, gives this stern warning:

> You shall not wrong or oppress a resident alien, for you were aliens in the land of Egypt. You shall not abuse any widow or orphan. If you do abuse them, when they cry out to me, I will surely heed their cry; my wrath will burn, and I will kill you with the sword, and your wives shall become widows and your children orphans. (Exodus 22:21-24)

To inspire strength and courage, the Bible tells of many ordinary women who rose to the occasion and became heroines, prophets, and even saviors. Furthermore, some of them happened to be migrants and foreigners. We shall examine several of them to demonstrate that these immigrant women of the Bible are clever, brave, resilient, and unrelenting in the pursuit of justice.

Shiphrah and Puah

It's possible that many people have never heard of Shiphrah and Puah. They were Hebrew midwives in the days when the Israelites were in Egypt (see Exodus 1). A new Pharaoh came to power who did not know Joseph, who had saved Egypt from a severe famine. Seeing that the Israelites had grown exponentially in numbers and strength, Pharaoh became afraid that they might try to take over the whole country; thus, he oppressed the Israelites and made them work like slaves. He even ordered the Hebrew midwives to kill all the Hebrew boys when they were born. However, Shiphrah and Puah disobeyed Pharaoh's order and allowed the boys to live for fear of God. When Pharaoh confronted them, they made up this tale saying, "Because the Hebrew women are not like the Egyptian women; for they are vigorous and give birth before the midwife comes to them" (Exodus 1:19). Shiphrah and Puah demonstrated bravery and strength in the face of grave danger from a powerful king. They chose to do the right thing by following God rather than obeying a wicked human ruler. Their act of "civil disobedience" (the earliest one recorded in the Bible) saved many children. We are told that God blessed them for their courage and obedience (Exodus 1:22).

Esther

Here is another remarkable immigrant woman who put her own life at risk to save her people. Esther was a young orphaned Jewish woman who lived in Babylon during the time of the Babylonian Exile. After the death of Esther's father and mother, her cousin Mordecai, who worked in the king's palace, took her in and raised her as his own daughter. While in search for a wife, the king laid eyes on Esther and was immediately captivated by her beauty. She won his favor and approval more than any other women in the royal court, and he chose Esther to be the queen. Haman, one of the king's advisors, didn't like Mordecai, partly because he was a Jew, and thus plotted to kill all the Jews in the empire. Mordecai discovered Haman's evil plot and convinced Esther to inform the king about it. Faced with danger and even the possibility of death, she prayed and fasted for three days and found the courage to approach the king. She told the king about her Jewish ancestry, revealed Haman's genocidal plot, and pleaded for her people. The king was impressed by her honesty and courage and ordered Haman to be hanged.

In the face of danger, Esther placed her trust in God and demonstrated remarkable strength to save the entire nation of Israel from being destroyed. Her inspiring example is still celebrated by Jews during Purim, which is a Jewish holiday that commemorates the deliverance of the Jewish people as told in the book that bears her name—Esther.

Ruth (and Naomi)

Our third example is Ruth. When talking about Ruth, we must also include Naomi. Naomi, her husband, and her two sons left Bethlehem because of a famine and settled in the land of Moab, which was located on the eastern side of the Dead Sea (Jordan today). In this foreign and enemy territory, Naomi's two boys married local girls. Tragedy struck, and Naomi's husband and two sons died in quick succession. It's unimaginable how Naomi must have felt.

Hearing that the famine was over in Israel, Naomi decided to return home to Bethlehem and suggested that her daughters-in-law stay behind and find new husbands. One did. Ruth however refused and insisted on accompanying Naomi until the end saying, "Do not press me to leave you or to turn back from following you! Where you go, I will go; where you lodge, I will lodge; your people shall be my people, and your God my God. Where you die, I will die—there will I be buried. May the Lord do thus and so to me, and more as well, if even death parts me from you!" (Ruth 1:16-17)

It's difficult to imagine what life was like for these two widows, one a migrant and the other a foreigner. Their situations were now reversed. Naomi, a humiliated migrant, had come home; Ruth, who had married a foreigner, had become a suspicious immigrant in a strange land. They struggled to survive. Ruth worked hard gleaning the fields to provide for herself and Naomi. Her hard work and reputation found favor with Naomi's kinsman Boaz. Boaz, the owner of the field that Ruth gleaned insisted that his workers leave a reasonable portion of the harvest for all the gleaners as dictated by the Law (see Deuteronomy 24:19; Leviticus 19:9-10). When he heard of the plight of his kin, Naomi and Ruth, Boaz offered them additional support.

Following the instructions of her mother-in-law, Ruth boldly claimed her levirate marriage right as prescribed by the Law (Deuteronomy 25:5). A levirate marriage is a type of marriage in which the brother of a deceased man is obliged to marry his brother's widow. The term levirate derives from the Latin word *levir*, meaning "husband's brother." Interestingly, Boaz accepted Ruth's request and followed all the appropriate procedures of the Law to secure Ruth as his rightful wife. Boaz acted with great kindness and decency. Ruth, equally admirable, remained loyal to Naomi and faithful to her promise to keep God's laws.

Who at that time could have guessed that a Moabite immigrant would affect the history of Israel's monarchy? Ruth gave birth to Obed, who was the grandfather of King David. Consequently, Ruth is the great-grandmother of Israel's most famous King. So noble was her character that she is included in the genealogy of the Messiah (Matthew 1:5). This is one more example of how nothing is impossible with God.

The Bible recounts many other remarkable women, for example, Eve, Sarah, Miriam, Deborah, Jael, Judith, Hannah, Mary, Elizabeth, Hagar, Anna, Martha, Mary Magdalene, Lydia, and Priscilla, just to name a few. Some were strong and brave women who led armies and challenged kings. Others were prophetesses who heard and obeyed the voice of God. Some were wise, making difficult decisions to help defeat their enemies and restore God's glory. Several of them even changed the course of history. Indeed, women, like men, are made in God's likeness and image (Genesis 1:27). They too are heirs to God's promise. For in Christ, according to St. Paul, there is no longer male or female (Galatians 3:28). In a patriarchal society, Paul's statement is profoundly radical.

Many biblical women were first and foremost mothers whose task was to protect their children. As a woman in a man's world, particularly widows and orphans without a man to rely on for protection, life could be difficult and precarious. Not surprisingly, the Bible has a lot to say about protecting these vulnerable individuals.

Protecting Our Children

Even in normal circumstances, children were already vulnerable. The infant mortality rate in first century Palestine was about 30 percent. Nearly a third of all babies died before the age of one. It is estimated that half of the children would not make it to the age of twelve. Being an infant in the time of Jesus was definitely a risky business. In times of war and violence, children suffered the most. Many became orphans. Others ended up as refugees, beggars, or slaves.

The children of our world today are also not free from danger and risk. In 2019, there were about 30 million children worldwide who became immigrants. An estimated 10 million were refugees who were forcibly displaced from their country, and another 17 million were internally displaced due to conflict and violence.[31] Many of these children were at grave risk of human trafficking, sexual violence, exploitation, family separation, and emotional trauma. All across the globe, millions of children are being uprooted, driven from their homes, deprived of education, and facing starvation.

In August 2017, a surge of violence began that forced about 1.2 million Rohingya refugees to leave Myanmar and cross the border into Bangladesh. About 60 percent or 683,000 of them were children.[32] Many of these Rohingya children walked for days to make it to already overcrowded makeshift refugee camps. They arrived exhausted, sick, and in desperate need of humanitarian assistance. The Rohingya are an ethnic group, mostly Muslims, who have lived in western Myanmar for centuries. Yet, they are stateless, unrecognized as citizens by the Myanmar government. Thus, they face discrimination, violence, and extreme poverty. Most of these children are deprived of education and are at real risk of becoming a "lost generation." Girls and women are at particular risk of sexual abuse and trafficking.

On the United States-Mexico border, the US Border Patrol apprehended nearly 69,000 unaccompanied children in 2014, 40,000 in 2015, and 60,000 in 2016. Sixty-one percent of these apprehended unaccompanied minors in 2016 were from El Salvador and Guatemala.[33]

Protecting those most vulnerable, particularly widows and orphans, is God's central concern. The Bible ensured their protection through legislation. The Torah states, "For the LORD your God is God of gods and Lord of lords, the great God, mighty and awesome, who is not partial and takes no bribe, who executes justice for the orphan and the widow, and who loves the strangers, providing them food and clothing" (Deuteronomy 10:17-18). The prophet Zechariah also exhorted the people of this time, reminding them that this is what God required of them saying, "Render true judgments, show kindness and mercy to one another; do not oppress the widow, the orphan, the alien, or the poor" (Zechariah 7:9-10). In the New Testament, James points out that there is a deep connection between faith and action stating, "Religion that is pure and undefiled before God, the Father, is this: to care for orphans and widows in their distress" (James 1:27). Jesus of course was also very protective of children.

"Let the Little Children Come to Me"

Jesus' famous words, "Let the little children come to me," can be found in all three Synoptic Gospels (Mark 10:14; Matthew 19:14; Luke 18:16). While this is a relatively simple phrase, it profoundly reveals Jesus' affection for children. It is appropriate to cite the whole passage found in Mark, the earliest Gospel:

> People were bringing little children to him in order that he might touch them; and the disciples spoke sternly to them. But when Jesus saw this, he was indignant and said to them, "Let the little

children come to me; do not stop them; for it is to such as these that the kingdom of God belongs. Truly I tell you, whoever does not receive the kingdom of God as a little child will never enter it." And he took them up in his arms, laid his hands on them, and blessed them. (Mark 10:13-16)

On another occasion, an argument started among the disciples as to which of them would be the greatest. Jesus, knowing their thoughts, placed a little child by his side and said to them, "Whoever welcomes this child in my name welcomes me" (Luke 9:48). Children are precious gifts from God. We must do everything possible to protect and nurture them. There are dire consequences for neglecting and mistreating them. Jesus says, "Take care that you do not despise one of these little ones; for, I tell you, in heaven their angels continually see the face of my Father in heaven" (Matthew 18:10).

Jesus didn't just talk about protecting children; he demonstrated it in his actions. Some notable examples of Jesus healing children are:

- Curing the daughter of a foreign woman (Mark 7: 24-30; Matthew 15:21-28);
- Curing a Roman soldier's son (John 4:46-50);
- Casting a demon out of a boy (Mark 9:14-29);
- Raising a girl (Mark 5:41-42) and a boy (Luke 7:11-17) to life;
- Curing a centurion's servant (Luke 7:1-10).

Compassion

The disturbing ordeals of women and children across the globe today should cause all of us to feel "compassion" as Jesus had often felt. The Greek word for compassion is *splanchnizomai*, which is literally translated "to be moved in one's bowels or in the inward parts"; hence, to feel compassion is to be moved so deeply by something that one feels it in the pit of one's stomach. This Greek word is frequently used to describe Jesus' emotion that almost always led him to action (for example, Mark 1:41; 6:34; Matthew 9:36; 14:14; etc.).

The Latin root for the word "compassion" is *compati*, which literally means "to suffer with." However, compassion is much more than just feeling sympathy or even empathy with someone's suffering. Compassion prompts a person to act on someone's behalf. That is why the Merriam-Webster Dictionary defines compassion as "the sympathetic consciousness of others' distress together with a desire to alleviate it." Taking action or getting involved to do something about a distressful situation is what separates compassion from sympathy and empathy. Having genuine compassion changes the way we live and affects the world around us. We must never remain silent in the face of injustice but act in the way the Bible beckons us: "Speak up for those who cannot speak for themselves, for the rights of all who are destitute. Speak up and judge fairly; defend the rights of the poor and needy" (Proverbs 31:8-9, NIV).

For Reflection:

- How do you feel when you hear about the sad ordeals of women and children today? Do they cause you enough "compassion" to want to do something about it? If so, what would it be?

- Which one of the strong immigrant women of the Bible impresses you the most? What are some of her strengths and traits that you wish to emulate?

Chapter Eight

Good Fences Make Good Neighbors?

Walls can be useful at times. They can provide a safe enclosure for children and pets and protection from dangerous people and animals. But walls can be a sign of something else—an exclusivity borne of privilege or fear.

In Robert Frost's classic poem, "Mending Wall,"[34] a man tells an apple farmer that the two of them must maintain a boundary between their orchards. With a stone firmly grasped in his hands, he declares, "Good fences make good neighbors." The apple farmer, a bit uneasy about the whole idea, responds, "Before I built a wall I'd ask to know / What I was walling in or walling out, / And to whom I was like to give offence." The farmer continues saying, "Something there is that doesn't love a wall, / That wants it down."

There is something in me also that dislikes a wall. My first experience of seeing a wall being put up happened just outside my window in East Jerusalem. In 2007, while directing a study tour in the Holy Land (Israel-Palestine), I stayed with the Comboni Missionary Sisters who have a house of hospitality in Bethany, about two miles east of Jerusalem on the slopes of the Mount of Olives. It is also known as *al-Eizariya* (Arabic for "Village of Lazarus"), which is now marked by the infamous "Security Wall," constructed by Israel since 2002. This fortified barrier stretches more than 400 miles, annexing Palestinian land inside the occupied West Bank. Depending on your perspective, the wall can mean different things. For Israelis, it has offered an understandable measure of security in a volatile region. Palestinians view it very differently. They refer to it as the "Separation Wall," the "Apartheid Wall," or simply "The Wall." As large slabs of grey concrete barriers twenty-eight feet high were being erected outside my window, I heard women crying uncontrollably. The Wall had cut across the Sisters' property separating them from their Palestinian neighbors and friends. Their cries of sadness reminded me of Rachel who mourned the loss of her children (Matthew 2:18; Jeremiah 31:15).

The Wall has a sobering effect on anyone who comes near it. Palestinians who live inside the wall, the "occupied territory," are isolated and feel imprisoned. Residents of Bethlehem, which is barely three miles away, need special permits and must deal with multiple checkpoints to enter Jerusalem. For Israelis, the wall offers protection against terrorism, which too often threatened daily life. A wall may be useful in some circumstances, but it is hardly an ideal, as it impedes human interrelationships.

Walls Throughout the Ages

Border fences and walls have been constructed throughout history to separate warring nations, protect trade routes, and deter migrants and refugees. At the end of World War II, there were less than ten known border walls in the world. By the time the Berlin Wall fell in 1989, the number had grown to fifteen. Today, there are at least seventy-seven such walls or fences around the world. Many were erected after terrorists attacked the US on September 11, 2001.[35]

The Great Wall of China, built more than 2,000 years ago, is often considered the longest feat of human engineering. It is more than 13,000 miles long and took untold numbers of workers to build. The US-Mexico border, the tenth longest in the world, extends 1,954 miles. While only a small portion of the border wall has been constructed, the US administration in 2016-20 planned to complete the border fence no matter the cost. There were even talks about installing floating border barriers to prevent migrants from trying to cross over the Rio Grande River that separates Mexico and the US.[36]

The Bible knows walls as well. The oldest protective wall known in human history was constructed at Jericho around 8,000 BC. This wall, which was made of stones, was about 12 feet high and 6 feet wide. The destruction of this oldest wall in the world is recorded in the Book of Joshua.

"The Walls Came Tumbling Down"[37]

Jericho is a famous biblical city located in the modern-day West Bank. Jesus passed through Jericho on his way to Jerusalem (Mark 10:46-52; Luke 19:1-10). Jericho was one of the earliest human settlements, dating back to the ninth-millennium BC. At around 1,400 BC, Jericho was the first city that the Israelites encountered after they had crossed the Jordan River and entered the Promised Land. Up until this point, according to the Bible, the Israelites had spent forty years wandering in the desert. Now they were face to face with the wall of Jericho that was tall and impenetrable. Joshua writes, "Jericho was shut up inside and out because of the Israelites; no one came out and no one went in" (6:1).

With the gates of the wall tightly shut, the Israelites were immobilized. God instructed Joshua to employ an unusual strategy to breach the wall and capture the city. Joshua and the Israelites followed God's instructions by marching around the city and carrying the Ark of the Covenant once a day for six straight days. On the seventh day, they marched around the wall of Jericho seven times blowing their trumpets and shouting in a loud voice, and the wall fell down. Only Rahab, a Canaanite woman who had sheltered some Israelite spies, and all those who belonged to her were spared. If the biblical story is accurate, then this event happened in the mid-to-late thirteenth century BC.

Archaeological excavations at the Tell es-Sultan in Jericho have failed to substantiate the biblical version of the destruction of its walls and conquest of the city. Biblical archaeologists have demonstrated that there was a destruction that occurred around 1500 BC during an Egyptian military campaign. Evidence or lack thereof seems to indicate that Jericho had been deserted or unoccupied from the late fifteenth century until the early tenth century BC, the supposed time of Joshua's conquest. Apparently the capture of Jericho as told in the Book of Joshua was not meant to be taken literally. It had symbolic value. The wall could not block Israel from receiving the land God had promised them.

How the Israelites came to settle in the Promised Land was a long and complex process that probably involved three types of events: military conquest, peaceful infiltration through migration, and peasant uprising. History teaches us that walls do not crumble easily. Protective walls, like those between Israel and the West Bank or the US and Mexico, are usually thick and heavily reinforced. However, walls do collapse just like parts of the Great Wall of China and the Berlin Wall. Nothing lasts forever. Besides, in the age of airplanes and satellites, walls no longer serve defensive purposes like they used to. Statistics have shown that most illegal immigrants in the US entered legally by way of airports on student, tourist, or work visas and then stayed past their visa's expiration date. It is estimated that visa overstays in the US have outnumbered illegal border crossings by a ratio of about two to one.[38]

Jericho was certainly not the only city that had a wall. Most ancient cities were built on a strategic location and fortified with protective walls and gates (Deuteronomy 3:5). This was a necessary means of survival, especially in a time of war. Jerusalem, for example, was a city surrounded by walls since ancient times. Here is how a psalmist describes the Holy City:

> I was glad when they said to me,
> "Let us go to the house of the LORD!"
> Our feet are standing within your gates,
> O Jerusalem.

Jerusalem—built as a city
   that is bound firmly together.

Pray for the peace of Jerusalem:
   "May they prosper who love you.

Peace be within your walls, and security
   within your towers." (Psalm 122:1-3, 6-7)

Jerusalem—A Citadel with Walls

King David captured Jerusalem from the Jebusites and made it the capital of his kingdom. Solomon, David's son, built the First Temple there on the hilltop and extended the city walls in order to protect the sacred Temple. During the siege in 587 BC, led by Nebuchadnezzar of Babylon, the walls and entire city were destroyed. After the Babylonian Exile, King Cyrus of Persia allowed the Jews to return to Judea and rebuild the Temple, known as the Second Temple. But it was Ezra and Nehemiah (in the late fifth century BC) who fortified the city with protective walls. During the Hasmonean period (second century BC) and the time of Herod the Great (37-4 BC) the city walls of Jerusalem were renovated and expanded.

In 70 AD, as a result of the Roman siege during the First Jewish-Roman War, the walls were almost completely destroyed. Jerusalem remained in ruins for some six decades and without protective walls for over two centuries. In the sixteenth century AD, during the Ottoman Empire, Sultan Suleiman the Magnificent decided to fully rebuild the city walls, partly on the remains of the ancient walls. They are the walls that exist presently. Visitors to the Old City of Jerusalem today can walk on most of the ancient city's walls via a Ramparts Walk.

Sadly, the walls of Jerusalem were not the only barriers that separated people from people in the time of Jesus. The Temple, which was the central place of Israel's cultic worship, was quite segregated. Although scholars debate the time frame for the establishment of these barriers, there is reason to believe some existed in Jesus' day.

A Temple with Many "Keep Out" Signs

Eighteen years into his reign as the Judean client-king of the Roman Empire, Herod the Great, who as an Idumean was considered only half-Jewish, began his greatest building project, which was a massive addition to the Temple of Jerusalem. The construction took several decades to complete. The Temple and other ambitious building projects, all of which were gigantic, earned him the epithet "the Great."

In the time of Jesus, the Temple was already the crowning jewel for the Jews and the hub of the region's economic activity. It was the center of wealth, commerce, and power, and served as an important symbol of national unity. As a faithful Jew, Jesus likely visited the Temple on numerous occasions, especially major feasts (John 2:13; 10:22-23). The Temple however comprised many subdivisions and restrictions on who could enter and in what area.

The outermost area of the Temple was the court of the Gentiles. It was the largest of all the courts accessible to all people: Jews, foreigners, and the ritually impure. Here, one could exchange money and buy animals for sacrifice. The "Beautiful Gate" (Acts 3:2, 10), which was decorative and huge, was the entrance to the court of women. This was the place where Israelite women could worship God in Jerusalem. Beyond the women's court, one passed through the Nicanor Gate into the innermost courts of the Temple. The first was the court of the men of Israel, and next to it was the court of the Priests. Beyond that court was the Sanctuary or Holy of Holies. Here, no one was allowed to enter except the High Priest, who could only go in once a year on Yom Kippur or the Day of Atonement. Though scholars differ on dating these practices, the Temple's many boundaries seemingly reflected the hierarchal structure of the day.

The first-century Roman-Jewish historian Josephus mentions a stone partition or railing about four and a half feet high surrounding the Temple proper. There were posted inscriptions or signs written in Greek and Latin warning Gentiles to keep out and not go any further, under pain of death. These "Do Not Enter" signs read: "No Gentile shall enter inward of the partition and barrier surrounding the Temple, and whomsoever is caught shall be responsible to himself for his subsequent death." Two of these Temple Warning Inscriptions were found and are now displayed in the Istanbul Archaeology Museums and the Israel Museum.

Interestingly, St. Paul was arrested because they thought that he had brought Greeks into the Temple area and thus defiled it (Acts 21:28-29). It is likely that Paul himself made a direct reference to the partitioning wall surrounding the Temple in his letter to the Ephesians. Paul talks about how the Gentiles were once strangers to the covenants of promise because they did not know God. Now in Christ Jesus, those who were once far off have been brought near by the blood of Christ. Paul wrote: "For he is our peace; in his flesh he has made both groups into one and has broken down the *dividing wall*, that is, the hostility between us" (Ephesians 2:14). A few verses later, Paul continues, saying, "So then you are no longer *strangers* and *aliens*, but you are citizens with the saints and also members of the household of God, built upon the foundation of the apostles and prophets, with Christ Jesus himself as the cornerstone" (Ephesians 2:19-20, italics added for emphasis).

Jesus—A Radical Prophet

Jesus of Nazareth was born and brought up in a specific culture. He was a Jew who spoke Palestinian Aramaic, likely read Hebrew and Greek, and was conditioned by a Semitic way of thinking and acting. One must realize that Jesus dressed, prayed, and taught like a Jew. His life, mission, and message were steeped in his Jewishness. As a faithful and pious Jew, Jesus acted with kindness and compassion to all people without distinctions. He also possessed a broad vision of the universality of humankind, already evident in some of the Jewish prophets before him, like Isaiah and Jeremiah.

We are told that Jesus travelled to Gentile territories on several occasions. He apparently crossed borders. It is reported that Jesus ventured into the region of Tyre and Sidon, and there he cured the daughter of a Canaanite woman who demonstrated "great faith" (Matthew 15:21-28). He traversed over to the other side of the Sea of Galilee into Gerasene territory (part of the ten Greek city states called the "Decapolis") and healed a demoniac possessed man (Mark 5:1-20). In the Gospel of John, Jesus often passes through Samaria, and on one occasion he engaged in a long conversation with a Samaritan woman and then accepted her and the Samaritans' hospitality (John 4). He also crossed more than literal borders; he frequently socialized with tax collectors and sinners. He touched and healed people who were considered ritually unclean, like lepers, or allowing the woman with the hemorrhage to touch him. One of the ten lepers he cured was a Samaritan (Luke 17:11-19).

When Jesus entered the Temple and saw the commotion and possibly the dividing wall, he became quite angry, overturning tables and protesting their business activities. The text does not say why he was infuriated, but the issue seems to have been about the desire to reestablish the Temple as "a house of prayer *for all the nations,*" not a "den of robbers" (Mark 11:17, italics for emphasis). What Jesus did in the Temple and being accused of speaking against it (Mark 15:58) probably cost him his life. It seemed that Jesus had envisioned a Temple that was supposed to be inclusive and unrestrictive, a place for all nations to come together. This attitude was in line with some prophetic teachings that called Israel to authentic worship, which was always the main goal of the Temple (Hosea 6:6; Jeremiah 7:1-4; Matthew 9:13). This radical vision of such a place is described in the Book of Revelation.

Vision of the New Jerusalem

The prophet John, who was exiled on the island of Patmos, was given a special vision of a new heaven and a new earth. John saw "the holy city, new Jerusalem, coming down out of heaven from God" (Revelation 21:1-2). In the new Jerusalem, there is no Temple since God and the Lamb are the Temple; there is no need of sun or moon, for the glory of God and the Lamb are its light and lamp; there is no need for locked gates, for only those who are righteous and pure may enter it (21:22-27). Those who are consecrated are no longer limited to Israel but are from all the nations—a new chosen race that is inclusive and universal. Even foreigners stream to the holy city (21:24, 26). John's vision of God's future home on earth is filled with life (22:1-2) and joy (22:3), so transforming and radical as to be a "new creation" or "new center" that does not marginalize anyone because of race, ethnicity, gender, or class. John's vision is not totally new, for the prophet Isaiah had already envisioned a similar world order (Isaiah 65:17-25).

The Pontiff on Building Bridges Not Walls

The word "pontiff" is derived from the Latin *pontifex*, which means "bridge-builder." True to his title as the Pontiff of the Catholic Church, Pope Francis has made it clear that as Christians we are to build bridges, not walls. The issue is not about legitimate security measures but about avoiding barriers to human interrelationships. In 2016, Pope Francis responded to the challenge of migration and to politicians who proposed building border fences, saying, "A person who thinks only of building walls, wherever they may be, and not building bridges, is not Christian. This is not the gospel."[39]

The Pope's comment aboard his flight from Mexico to Rome sparked controversy across the globe. Since that famous interview, the Pope has continued to speak out against governments that build walls to keep out migrants and refugees. He has appealed for a compassionate approach to migration. On March 31, 2019, aboard another flight from Morocco to Rome, the Pope said, "The builders of walls with blades that cut, with knives or with bricks, will become prisoners of the walls they make. History tells us that."[40]

For Reflection:

- Do you have a wall around your house or wherever you live? What or who is it walling in or walling out? To whom might it cause offense?

- How do you feel about Pope Francis' comment that the person who builds walls and not bridges is not a Christian? Furthermore, what kind of walls (e.g., racism, sexism, ageism, etc.) do we unknowingly construct to block people out?

Chapter Nine

Legal and Illegal Migration:
What Difference Does It Make?

For many years, I was regarded as an "alien." Since I was a foreign-born person who was not a US citizen but was legally recorded as a resident of the country, I was labeled as a "resident alien." As a child, I couldn't understand why I was designated that way. Where I came from we had coconut trees and beautiful beaches. Sure, we ate mangos and plenty of fish, but why that made me an "alien" was beyond my comprehension as a ten-year old boy who had just arrived on these strange shores of the United States of America.

It is estimated that more than 1 million "resident aliens" arrive in the US each year. These foreign-born individuals are lawfully recognized as residents of the country and allowed to live and work even though they are not US citizens. As legal immigrants, they must have a green card or pass a substantial presence test. They are also subject to the same taxes as other US citizens. There are other terms that may be used to identify the status of a resident alien. The following identifications, which are more precise and politically correct, are used interchangeably: legal immigrant, permanent resident, or green card holder. In 2018, there were about 44.8 million legal immigrants living in the US. Approximately one in seven US residents was foreign born.[41]

While an exact number is impossible to determine, the number of undocumented immigrants living in the US ranged from 10.5 to 12 million in 2019.[42] Undocumented immigrants are foreign-born people who do not possess a valid visa or other immigration documentation, because they entered the US without inspection, stayed longer than their temporary visa permitted, or otherwise violated the terms under which they were admitted. A person entering or remaining in the US without valid documentation is in violation of federal immigration laws. These folks are often labeled as "illegal aliens." In 2016, the Library of Congress announced that it would use "non-citizens" or "unauthorized immigrants" as a bibliographical term, rather than calling them "illegal aliens." This once common designation had become offensive. Unfortunately, this unpleasant identification persists among top politicians and continues to appear in many official documents and government websites, for example, those of the White House.[43]

Illegal immigration is a matter of intense debate in the US and in many parts of the world. How should Christians respond to this extremely controversial and volatile issue? Intriguingly, there is fervent claim of biblical support on both sides.

The Rights of Sovereign Nations

The immigration debate is complex. Among the many issues involved, two are most contentious. First, those who immigrate to the US, for example, without going through the proper legal channels are here illegally and therefore are "illegal immigrants." According to some, these people should be labeled as such and not the euphemistic "undocumented immigrants." Furthermore, these immigrants should have no expectations that their lives here should be the same as for those who are legal citizens. They broke the law to come here and should expect to be deported by the office of Immigration and Customs Enforcement (ICE). This side of the debate strongly advocates for immigration reform that would not favor a path to legal status and citizenship for illegal/undocumented immigrants.

Second, the immigration debate centers on the issue of borders. There are those who advocate for an open border policy, fully or conditionally.[44] The US is a nation built by immigrants. A core American value is that everyone has a chance to succeed because, as long as you work hard, you will find a place in this country. Constructing a wall at the border denies this basic principle and is therefore un-American. Opponents of fully open borders have argued that this view is crazy and senseless because according to President Donald Trump, "A nation without borders is not a nation."[45] In January 2017, President Trump signed two executive orders related to immigration and border security, moving ahead with his plans to build a wall along the US border with Mexico and to deport people who were in the country illegally. This view is based on the typical image of immigrants sneaking across the US-Mexican border. But only about half of the undocumented immigrants arrive this way. The other half, less noted and rarely making the headline news, arrive legally, typically on work, tourist, or student visas, but then overstay their visa status.

National sovereignty is the heart of the immigration debate. For many Christians, the idea of a sovereign nation enforcing its own immigration policy and protecting its borders does not contradict the teaching of Scripture. Proponents of this position usually turn to the Apostle Paul to back up their claim. Paul writes, "Let every person be subject to the governing authorities; for there is no authority except God, and those authorities that exist have been instituted by God. Therefore whoever resists authority resists what God has appointed, and those who resist will incur judgment" (Romans 13:1-2). He instructed Christians to submit to government and obey the law of the land. Accordingly, those who cross a nation's border illegally have broken a government's law, and so have committed a sin.

Similarly, the author of First Peter urged the "aliens and exiles" of his time to "accept the authority of every human institution, whether of the emperor as supreme, or of governors, as sent by him to punish those who do wrong and to praise those who do right" (2:11 ,13-14). As instructed by Holy Scripture, Christians should obey the laws of a sovereign nation. Thus, supporting, enabling, and/or encouraging illegal immigration is a violation of God's Word.

Interestingly, the Church does not oppose the right of sovereign nations to control their borders and territories. However, it also recognizes the right of people to migrate when it is necessary. The pastoral letter concerning migration from the Catholic Bishops of Mexico and the US, "Strangers No Longer, Together on the Journey of Hope" (2003), states:

> The Church recognizes the right of a sovereign state to control its borders in furtherance of the common good. It also recognizes the right of human persons to migrate so that they can realize their God-given rights. These teachings complement each other. While the sovereign state may impose reasonable limits on immigration, the common good is not served when the basic human rights of the individual are violated.[46] (number 39)

Realizing the danger of branding all undocumented immigrants as "rapists and drug traffickers," Pope Francis called on the US and the world to adopt a humanitarian approach to those crossing borders, especially children. The Pope said at a global conference in Mexico in 2014, "Many people forced to emigrate suffer, and often, die tragically; many of their rights are violated, they are obligated to separate from their families and, unfortunately, continue to be the subject of racist and xenophobic attitudes."[47]

The Pope was keenly aware that stereotypes and myths about immigrants perpetuate xenophobic attitudes and are often used as a basis for policy decisions around the issues of legal and illegal migration.

Myths Perpetuate Xenophobia

Stereotypes and myths about migration do greatly influence people's views. These myths can heighten xenophobia and cause tension, violence, and unrest. There are many myths about undocumented immigrants. Among the notable ones are: they are overrunning the country; they steal jobs; they drain the country's social assistance, education, and healthcare services; they don't pay taxes; and building a wall across the Mexican border will stop illegals and terrorists from entering the US. Facts have shown that these views are pure myths and are not true.[48]

Research has shown that undocumented immigrants contribute to economic growth, enhance the welfare of the natives, pay more in tax revenue than they collect, and benefit consumers by reducing the prices of goods and services. Statistics have indicated that immigrants commit less crime than natives.[49]

Misconceptions and myths have greatly fueled xenophobia, a fear or hatred of anything strange or foreign, particularly as it relates to people. Anti-immigrant rhetoric and movements are on the rise around the world. Regrettably, xenophobic attitudes also appear on the pages of the Bible.

Anti-Immigrant Sentiments

For the most part, the Bible is quite favorable towards immigrants. There was, however, a period in Israel's history when several biblical characters were unequivocally anti-foreigner. After the Persians had defeated the Babylonian Empire, the captive Israelites were allowed to return home to Judea to rebuild Jerusalem and the Temple. Two famous returnees contributed greatly to the restoration. Under the military leadership of Nehemiah, the walls of Jerusalem were rebuilt and fortified, providing security and protection. The priest Ezra restored the Jewish cultic and religious life. Both Nehemiah and Ezra (around 350-300 BC) helped rebuild a fractured community and established a spiritual cohesion. In order to avoid the sins of the past and prevent another exile, they called for a purification of the people. To maintain their status as a people set apart for God, they began to purge anything that was brought in from the outside. Foreigners were deemed unclean and considered a threat to the establishment. With heightened concern for ritual purity, typically advocated by the priesthood to maintain Jewish identity in a secular environment, contact with foreigners could dilute such identity. Ezra was greatly concerned about "the holy seed" having "mixed itself with the peoples of the lands" (Ezra 9:2). Thus, Ezra the priest instructed the people saying:

> You have trespassed and married foreign women, and so increased the guilt of Israel. Now make confession to the Lord the God of your ancestors, and do his will; separate yourselves from the peo-

ples of the land and from the foreign wives. Then all the assembly answered with a loud voice, "It is so; we must do as you have said." (Ezra 10:10-12)

Nehemiah instituted a similar policy prohibiting intermarriages and even imposed cruel punishment on violators (Nehemiah 9:2; 13:25). In the context of the post-exilic period, the returnees needed cohesion. Furthermore, to remain pure and faithful to the covenant, they felt that it was necessary to reject anything that was foreign. These "foreigners" or "aliens" whom the Israelites had to avoid were called *nokhrim* in Hebrew, appearing only nineteen times in the Bible (for example, Ezra 10:2, 10, 14, 17, 44; Nehemiah 13:26). The Canaanites, Moabites, or Amorites were called *nokhrim*. These foreigners had no rights or privileges in the Israelite community and were to be shunned at all cost.

At the same time, however, there were other biblical authors who portrayed the foreigners in a completely different light. The Books of Jonah and Ruth, for example, challenged the anti-foreign stance of Ezra and Nehemiah. The prophet Jonah was commanded to go to the Ninevites, Israel's despised enemies, to offer them God's mercy and redemption (see chapter ten). The story of Ruth celebrated the loyalty of a Moabite woman who followed her mother-in-law Naomi back to Israel and accepted Israel's God as her own (see chapter seven). The author of Isaiah 56-66 (known as Third-Isaiah) envisioned a future gathering of both Israelites and foreigners on Zion, the holy mountain, worshiping the one true God (Isaiah 56:1-8). Interestingly, Isaiah also called these "foreigners" *nokhrim*. These were

people from other lands who would come before the LORD, echoing the hope of Solomon in First Kings 8:41-43, whereby foreigners and Israelites together would enjoy God's presence in a glorious fashion.

The authors of the Bible, just like most people today, did not share the same theology or public policy. Nevertheless, the overwhelming evidence suggests that a coherent theology and biblical position demands a pro-immigrant stance. This is most forthright in Israel's laws.

Laws Favoring the Immigrants

Throughout the Old Testament legal teaching, the Israelites are constantly reminded to care for the strangers, migrants, and refugees because they were once foreigners in the land of Egypt. The author of Deuteronomy exhorts:

> For the LORD your God is God of gods and Lord of lords, the great God, mighty and awesome, who is not partial and takes no bribe, who executes justice for the orphan and the widow, and who loves the strangers, providing them food and clothing. You shall also love the stranger, for you were strangers in the land of Egypt. (10:17-19)

The Book of Leviticus issues a similar commandment:

> When an alien resides with you in your land, you shall not oppress the alien. The alien who resides with you shall be to you as the citizen among

you; you shall love the alien as yourself, for you were aliens in the land of Egypt: I am the LORD your God. (19:33-34)

Inspired by the memory of Israel's past, the Old Testament legal statutes made sure that the rights of the immigrants were recognized and upheld.[50] In terms of social rights, the immigrants (*gerim* in Hebrew) were given the same legal privileges as the native Israelites in the following situations:

- seeking asylum (Numbers 35:15),

- protection from oppression (Exodus 22:20; Leviticus 19:33-34),

- receiving an annual portion of the tithe (Deuteronomy 14:28-29),

- gleaning rights (Deuteronomy 24:19; Leviticus 19:10), and

- receiving equal justice before a judge (Deuteronomy 1:16; 24:17).

As for religious rights, the immigrants were allowed to participate in the following cultic activities and ceremonies:

- observance of the Sabbath (Exodus 20:10; Deuteronomy 5:14),

- renewal of the covenant (Deuteronomy 29:10-11),

- participation in the various Jewish Feasts: Weeks (Deuteronomy 16:11), Tabernacles (Deuteronomy

16:14), Passover (Exodus 12:48-49), and the Day of Atonement (Leviticus 16:29-30).

On the part of immigrants residing in the land of Israel, the following expectations and responsibilities were required of them:

- be present at the periodic reading of the Law (Deuteronomy 31:10-13),

- be subject to the penalties of criminal laws (Leviticus 24:21-22),

- observe dietary restrictions (Exodus 12:19; Leviticus 17:10-15) and purity laws (Numbers 19:10),

- avoid sexual taboos (Leviticus 18:26),

- refrain from worshiping other gods and blaspheming against the LORD (Leviticus 20:1-2; Numbers 15:30-31).

In general, the laws of the Old Testament were uniquely gracious to immigrants because no other ancient Near Eastern law codes had such instructions. The incentive or motivation to care for the strangers must have come from Israel's collective memory of how God had cared for them when they were estranged, oppressed, and vulnerable. Israel, too, was to love strangers, migrants, and refugees because God does (Psalm 146:6-9). Neglecting justice for these people is a sin (Deuteronomy 24:14-15).

The biblical command of being kind to immigrants is also binding today. Everyone is responsible to uphold this sacred directive, from individuals, to institutions, to society as a whole. This ethical mandate should especially resonate with Christians.

Encounter the Face of God

How should Christians respond to illegal immigrants? The same way we respond to anyone else—with mercy and love. Quoting the prophet Hosea, Jesus said, "I desire mercy, not sacrifice" (Matthew 9:13; Hosea 6:6). Another of his famous dictums was "Be merciful, just as your Father is merciful" (Luke 6:36). If you want to see the face of God, just examine Jesus' words and actions. Jesus is the face of God's mercy.

The world is witnessing an increasing level of violence, fear, and hatred that challenges us each day. Racial tensions continue to run high, particularly in the United States, with police killings and police brutality routinely making the news and social media. There are ongoing debates about illegal immigration and border security. News headlines of the plight of refugees around the world continue to pop up on our screens. In times like these, talk about mercy may seem unreal and impossible. But mercy does matter, now more than ever. At an Easter address and apostolic blessing (*Urbi et Orbi* — "to the city and the world"), Pope Francis said:

> God's mercy can make even the driest land become a garden, can restore life to dry bones

(cf. Ezekiel 37:1-14). ... Let us be renewed by God's mercy, let us be loved by Jesus, let us enable the power of his love to transform our lives too; and let us become agents of this mercy, channels through which God can water the earth, protect all creation and make justice and peace flourish.[51]

Mercy is love. Pope St. John Paul II said it so eloquently, "Mercy is really love transformed, so we need to understand what love is if we are to penetrate more deeply into what it means to be merciful."[52]

We are familiar with St. Paul's famous hymn of love in First Corinthians: "If I speak in the tongues of mortals and of angels, but do not have love, I am a noisy gong or a clanging cymbal. And if I have prophetic powers, and understand all mysteries and all knowledge, and if I have all faith, so as to remove mountains, but do not have love, I am nothing" (1 Corinthians 13:1-2). The author of the letters of John also exhorted his fellow Christians saying, "Beloved, let us love one another, because love is from God; everyone who loves is born of God and knows God. Whoever does not love does not know God, for God is love" (1 John 4:7-8).

Jesus Christ defines love in concrete actions, namely, when we feed the hungry, give water to the thirsty, welcome a stranger, clothe the naked, care for the sick, or visit the prisoner. "Truly I tell you," Jesus said, "just as you did it to one of the least of these who are members of my family, you did it to me" (Matthew 25:40).

In short, both Testaments call for a more demanding love of those whom we otherwise would consider outsiders.

For Reflection:

- Which stereotypes or myths about illegal immigrants have greatly fueled xenophobic attitudes leading to anti-immigrant rhetoric and policy among politicians and churchgoers?

- What is the difference between mercy and justice? Why is mercy such an important Christian value? Can a person be a true Christian without mercy?

Chapter Ten

Migrants as Missionaries

The island of Anguilla is a British overseas territory in the Eastern Caribbean, also referred to as the West Indies. Anguilla is one of the most northerly of the Leeward Islands, lying east of Puerto Rico and the Virgin Islands. It is a flat island of coral and limestone and is noted for its spectacular coral reefs and pristine beaches attracting many tourists. Consequently, the island's main source of revenue is tourism.

On this attractive vacation spot, so far removed from Asia, lives a small population of Catholic Filipinos. They, of course, did not come from the other side of the globe for a vacation but rather for labor. About a dozen of these Filipino migrant workers belong to the choir of St. Gerard's Roman Catholic Church. They actually established the Saturday choir and take charge of the music at every Sunday Vigil Mass. Some of them are married, but most are single. Their beautiful voices and upbeat songs, accompanied by drum and guitar, usually attract a good crowd. During the Communion meditation they normally sing a traditional Tagalog hymn to add more flavor to an already very cross-cultural liturgy. The members of the congregation are predominantly Caribbean with dark skin whose ancestors came from Africa. A few tourists from Europe or North America occasionally come to church. I, a visiting priest, who was born in Viet Nam but now live and work in the United States, was the main celebrant of the Mass.

As I looked across the pews and witnessed the migrant Filipino workers singing and praising God with fervent joy and enthusiasm "in a foreign land" (Psalm 137:4), I was greatly moved with admiration and compassion. As migrant workers they have taken their religion with them and fervently give witness to their faith in songs and by serving at their local church. Although vulnerable and displaced from their homeland and family, they actively live out their Christian faith, contributing much and becoming a precious gift to this small Catholic community.

Christianity – A Migratory Religion

Church historians have correctly noted that Christianity has been a migratory religion, and its migrants have helped the missionary expansion of the Church. From the very beginning, Christian expansion and migratory movement were forcibly and intimately intertwined. Human mobility was and remains a prime factor in the global spread of Christianity.

Reviewing the religious composition of international migrants, about 49 percent of all international migrants are Christians.[53] Statistics indicate that Christian migrants are the largest population on the move. The two favorite destinations of Christian migrants have been North America and Europe.[54] If every Christian migrant is a potential missionary, migration then could have enormous prospects and opportunities for evangelism. When Christians migrate, they take their religion with them, or more personally, their God literally moves with them. This of course is not new. Migration was already a key factor in the expansion of the Church in the New Testament times.

A Church in Motion and on a Mission

The Acts of the Apostles illustrates that migration and mission go hand in hand. Luke—who is also the author of Acts—recounts the origins and expansion of the Christian mission from Jerusalem to Rome. Defying all odds, the early followers of Jesus Christ brought the good news of salvation from "Jerusalem, in all Judea and Samaria, and to the ends of the earth" (Acts 1:8).

The age of the early church was the age of migration and mission under the guidance of the Holy Spirit. From beginning to end, Luke shows that the Holy Spirit directed and guided the work of salvation every step of the way, whether by design or force. Ironically, the persecutions of the Greek-speaking Jewish Christians (the "Hellenists") after Stephen's martyrdom (around 32 AD) and the killing of the apostle James (around 44 AD) led to various waves of migration. Christians moved from Jerusalem to the countryside of Judea and Samaria (Acts 8:1) and as far as to Phoenicia, Cyprus, and Antioch (11:19). The effect of migration was to give impetus to the Christian mission that reached out not only to Jews in the Diaspora but also to Gentiles.

Jonah—the Reluctant Missionary

The theme of mission to the nations is not exclusive to the New Testament but already found in the Old Testament. The prophet Jonah was commissioned by God to go to the people of Nineveh to prophesy against their wickedness and about their impending destruction if they did not change. Nineveh was the capital of the Assyrian Empire that had destroyed the northern kingdom of Israel and enslaved many Israelites. The Ninevites, therefore, were Israel's bitter enemies. It was no surprise that Jonah did not want to have anything to do with them.

After having been thrown into the sea and then swallowed by a large fish, Noah hesitantly obeyed God's command by going to Nineveh and announcing, "Forty days more, and Nineveh shall be overthrown!" (Jonah 3:4) All the inhabitants of the city heeded his words and repented. The king of Nineveh and even the animals put on sackcloth and sat in ashes to show their conversion. Thus, God relented in his initial intention to destroy the city and its inhabitants. Intriguingly, Jonah was greatly displeased and became angry with God for showing such mercy to these foreigners. Jonah admitted that God was being faithful to his own character saying, "I knew that you are a gracious God and merciful, slow to anger, and abounding in steadfast love, and ready to relent from punishing"

(Jonah 4:2). Jonah was directly quoting Exodus 34:6-7. Essentially, Jonah was angry with God because God had extended "steadfast love" (*hesed* in Hebrew) to outsiders. Jonah might have presumed that this kind of "covenantal love" was reserved only for the Israelites and not meant to be shared with others, particularly Israel's enemies.

Unlike Jonah, the earliest disciples of Jesus understood the importance of sharing the good news of mercy and salvation with all people. Peter and Paul, for example, took seriously Jesus' great commission: "Go, therefore and make disciples of all nations" (Matthew 28:19).

Peter and Paul—Apostles and Missionaries

As the apostle to the Jews and the pillar of the church in Jerusalem, Peter dominates the first half of Acts (chapters 1 to 12). Representing the Twelve, Peter was the primary witness to Jesus as Messiah and Lord in Jerusalem, Judea and Samaria. Having received the gift of the Holy Spirit, Peter boldly delivered the powerful mission sermon at Pentecost (Acts 2:14-41) and other evangelical speeches (3:12-26; 10:34-43), performed miraculous deeds (3:1-10; 5:12-16; 9:32-43), fearlessly confronted hostile opposition (4:18-20; 5:29-32), and endured flogging and imprisonment (5:18, 40-41; 12:3). Peter even courageously ventured into a Gentile territory—Caesarea—to deliver the message of salvation to a Roman centurion, Cornelius, and had table-fellowship with the Gentile soldier and his entire household. Peter's acts of testimony are hallmarks of "one sent" (*apostolos*) on mission in the name of the risen Christ.

Once the Gentile mission has been fully endorsed and authorized by the Jerusalem church (Acts 11:1-18; 15:1-35), Paul—the apostle to the Gentiles—takes the central stage of Acts (chapters 13 to 28) as the primary instrument of carrying the message of repentance and salvation to Galatia, Asia Minor, Greece, and finally to Rome. But to fulfill the missionary mandate of the risen Christ, the great apostle had to endure many trials and sufferings for the sake of Christ and the gospel. As one imbued with the fire of the Holy Spirit (Acts 9:17; 13:2-3), Paul ventured out into uncharted territory, establishing Christian communities in many towns and cities. Nothing could weaken his missionary zeal and spirit, not stoning (14:19), imprisonments (16:23; 28:30-31), physical torture and beatings (16:22-23; 22:22-30), constantly being chased away or pursued (13:50; 23:12-22), shipwreck (27:1-44), or interrogations (24:23-35; 26:1-32), just to name a few incidents (for a longer list of Paul's own testimony of sufferings see 2 Corinthians 11:21-28). His relentless determination to share the good news of the risen Christ altered the landscape of the Mediterranean basin within a short period of time.

Together in Mission

Peter and Paul of course did not and could not complete the mission by themselves. They relied on other apostles, co-workers, companions, friends, and associates. Peter was often accompanied by John (Acts 3:1, 11; 4:13, 19; 8:14). Paul depended upon a network of friends and co-workers: Barnabas (Acts 13:2); John Mark (12:25); Silas (15:22); Judas (15:22); Timothy (16:1); Apollos (18:24); and Luke (16:11). There were also women who worked alongside Paul and assisted him in his ministry. The first European convert was Lydia, a dealer in purple cloth, who migrated to Philippi from the city of Thyatira in western Asia Minor. After her conversion, Paul and his traveling companions frequented her home and were greatly encouraged by her generosity (16:15, 40). An outstanding couple worth highlighting is Priscilla and Aquila.

Priscilla and Aquila

The story of Priscilla and Aquila illustrates that migration and mission were closely intertwined.[55] This Judean-Christ-believing-couple was constantly on the move for the cause of the gospel. The references to Priscilla and Aquila appear six times in the New Testament: three times by Luke (Acts 18:1-3, 18-19, 26-27) and three times by Paul (1 Corinthians 16:19; Romans 16:3; 2 Timothy 4:19). They first settled in Rome, were then forced to migrate to Corinth because of the Edict of Claudius in 49 AD, relocated in Ephesus for the purpose of evangelization, and finally returned to Rome after Claudius' death in 54 AD. Their home was as movable as the tents that they erected. Even though they relocated both their home and their trade at least three times to three different locations (Rome, Corinth, and Ephesus), they never faltered in their commitment to preach the gospel of Jesus Christ, risking everything because of faith. Not surprisingly, Paul mentioned this couple in several letters giving them the highest honor and accolades by regarding them as "co-workers" and faithful friends who risked "their necks" for his life (Romans 16:3-5; 1 Corinthians 16:19; 2 Timothy 4:19).

Like any immigrant who experiences the trauma of displacement and marginalization, they knew the importance of being welcomed and finding shelter. Their homes became house churches. The case of Priscilla and Aquila is a good example for lay Christian immigrants scattered all over the globe to emulate, for their displacement, whether voluntary or involuntary, can serve as an opportunity for hospitality, mission, and evangelism. Furthermore, the story of Priscilla and Aquila also serves as a reminder for the Church to realize that Christian migrants, voluntary and involuntary, can fall within the plan of God and become a key factor in the expansion of the Church. Migrants can sometimes turn out to be angels in disguise.

Migrants as Precious Gifts of the Church

Christian migrants have precious gifts to give to the Church. Recognizing the "gift" of migrants, the Catholic Church continually seeks ways to appropriately address the needs and pastoral care of migrants and refugees. One of its pontifical documents states:

It should be led by the principle that no one, be
they migrants, refugees or members of the local
population, should be looked upon as a 'stranger,'
but rather as a 'gift,' in parishes and other ecclesial communities. This is an authentic expression
of the 'catholicity' of the Church.[56]

The church therefore has an obligation to care for and
equip them for mission.

On June 2, 2000, the Jubilee Day for Migrants and
Refugees, Pope John Paul II looked out over a sunlit crowd
of pilgrims gathered in St. Peter's Square from all nations:
migrants, refugees, seafarers, Gypsies, foreign students, circus
and carnival workers, airport workers, truckers, all varieties
of people on the move with their promoters and chaplains.
The Pope celebrated the Eucharist, which drew that great
diversity of people into unity in the communion of Father,
Son, and Holy Spirit. He reminded them that in the Church
they are meant to experience this Trinitarian communion.

This jubilee vision of Pope John Paul II has been the
vision guiding the bishops of the United States, as they
responded to the new immigrants who had recently come
to their shores. Many of the new immigrants are Catholics.
Probably more than 80 percent of Hispanic immigrants were
raised in the Catholic faith. By some estimates, Hispanic
Catholics will soon make up the majority of Catholics in
North America. But other immigrant populations also
include large numbers of Catholics. Filipinos, who represent almost 5 percent of the immigrant population, are
overwhelmingly Catholic. Some 350,000 of the 1.4 million

Vietnamese immigrants in this country are Catholic. These Catholics are joined by thousands of Eastern Catholics coming from the former Soviet Union, the Middle East, and India. A smaller but still significant number of the Chinese, Korean, Japanese, Laotian, Sri Lankan, Indonesian, Tongan, Samoan, and Asian Indian immigrants are also Catholic. Among the increasing numbers of immigrants from Africa, many are Catholics, raised in the vibrant Catholic culture of the Church's fastest growing region.[57]

Recognizing their precious gift to the U.S. Church, the Committee on Migration of the United States Conference of Catholic Bishops (USCCB) in 2001 wrote a wonderful document entitled, *Asian and Pacific Presence: Harmony in Faith*. This pastoral letter affirms with loving assurance their presence and prominence in the U.S. Catholic Church. It states: "We pray that this pastoral statement will facilitate a fuller appreciation of their communities in our local churches and will encourage Asian and Pacific Catholics to take on active leadership roles in every level of church life."[58] The document celebrates numerous gifts and contributions by which Asian and Pacific Catholics have enriched church communities over many decades.

A Marvelous Rainbow

We are living in a time when ethnic, cultural, and linguistic diversity is more evident and intense than ever. Like it or not, the face of the Church in the twenty-first century will continue to be even more ethnically diverse due to the worldwide phenomenon of migration. Unlike attitudes of the past, diversity is not a thing to overcome but rather an essential component to foster. This can be an hour of great opportunities for the Church and its evangelizing mission. At our Sunday celebrations, one cannot help but notice the cultural diversity of peoples represented in the pews. The Anglo, African, Asian and Hispanic faces form a magnificent rainbow of colors.

The face of the priesthood is also changing. On any given Sunday, thousands of foreign-born priests are preaching from the pulpit. While an exact count is not available, it is estimated that there are over 8,500 foreign-born priests currently serving in the U.S. Each year there are approximately 300 new international priests who come to North America to begin a new ministry. The majority of these foreign-born priests come from Asia, Africa, and Latin America.

Interestingly the U.S. Catholic Church is becoming a mission-receiving Church rather than a mission-sending Church. This is a clear sign of "mission-in-reverse." In the archdiocese of Los Angeles, for example, the Mass on any given weekend is conducted in forty-five different languages. Consequently, mono-cultural parishes are being replaced by "shared parishes" or "national parishes," that is parishes in which more than one language, racial or cultural group worship together as one Christian community.

As "shared," "national," or "multicultural" parishes become the norm, everyone must be prepared to embrace the reality of our Church and learn to appreciate its extraordinary variety. This is simply an extension of the biblical vision we have recounted above. Preachers, ministers and pastoral workers are especially encouraged to prepare themselves to work in diverse environments and to foster the right knowledge, attitudes and skills to be effective in the diverse vineyard of the Lord. Preaching and ministering in a cross-cultural context, particularly in the age of global migration, is no longer an option but a pastoral necessity.

For Reflection:

- If Christian migrants are the largest population on the move, and since every Christian migrant is a potential missionary, what does this mean for the prospects and opportunities for evangelization, and how should the Church respond to the new arrivals?

- The story of Priscilla and Aquila serves as a reminder for the Church to realize that Christian migrants, voluntary and involuntary, can fall within the plan of God and become a key factor in the expansion of the Church. Share an experience when a migrant turned out to be an angel in disguise.

Afterword

What this book has tried to show is that the Bible can indeed speak to the plight of strangers, immigrants, and refugees in our day. This is an immensely complex and highly controversial topic. Today's migration makes up the greatest movement of people of all time. This global phenomenon, caused by globalization, political and ethnic conflicts, environmental disasters, virus pandemics (like COVID-19), free trade, and viable means of transportation, has led more and more people to migrate than ever before. No continent, region, or country is immune from this worldwide crisis. Crossing international borders, or even moving around within a country, is a major characteristic of our present age. No wonder some call it "the age of migration."

True, this issue is not simple. There are ongoing debates about illegal immigration and border security. News of the predicament of refugees around the world continues to make headlines, almost daily. Regrettably, the world is witnessing an increasing level of anti-immigrant rhetoric and sentiments. Stereotypes and myths about immigrants have greatly fueled xenophobia and caused racial tension, violence, and unrest.

How should Christians respond to this adverse and troubled sign of the times? This book affirms that our inspiration and guidance can come from the Scriptures, both Old and New Testament, which we hold sacred—the living Word of God. For the most part, we saw that the Bible is very favorable toward immigrants, for much of it was written by, for, and about strangers, migrants, and refugees. From Genesis to Revelation, the Bible is really a tapestry woven together from the stories of one great migrant family. The entire Bible gives witness to the stories of so many of our ancestors of faith who were sojourners in foreign lands: Adam and Eve, Abraham and Sarah, Joseph and Moses, Ruth and Esther, Jesus himself and the all the early apostles, Peter and Paul, and important colleagues like Priscilla and Aquila. The history of Israel itself is the history of wandering and dispersion. It is also a story of faith in the God who accompanied them on their journey. They were never orphaned. We also saw that for Christians, migration and mission are closely intertwined. Like all Jesus' followers, we are sent forth. We cannot escape the fact that our background is filled with such immigrants and refugees from whom we can take inspiration.

Most biblical authors portray foreigners in a positive light. (Ezra and Nehemiah were exceptions, owing to their unique historical circumstances.) Not surprisingly, the Bible is essentially pro-immigrant because of Israel's own wanderings. This was also apparent in Israel's laws. In most social and cultic regulations, immigrants are given the same legal privileges as native Israelites. Yet we did not gloss over some nuances. Concerning walls and borders, for instance, the Bible acknowledges their usefulness, but one that separates village from village, discriminates people from people, or splits family from family is unwarranted. While the Bible does not oppose the right of sovereign nations to control their borders and territories, it also recognizes the right of people to migrate when necessary. In addition, we saw that the Bible has a lot to say about many issues related to migration, such as, human trafficking, refugees and asylum seekers, victims of war and violence, women and children, and climate change and natural disasters.

We need not be paralyzed by the complexities of these issues. In our day, when racial tensions and fear of foreigners continue to run high, particularly in the United States, we need to find the path our ancestors took: the path of mercy. Talk of mercy may seem unreal and impossible. But mercy matters, now more than ever. Mercy is love. And Jesus Christ is the face of God's love. Jesus defines love in concrete actions, namely, when one feeds the hungry, gives water to the thirsty, *welcomes a stranger*, clothes the naked, cares for the sick, or visits the prisoner. "Truly I tell you," Jesus said, "just as you did it to one of the least of these who are members of my family, you did it to me" (Matthew 25:40).

Since hospitality is love in action, it is the most appropriate response to the immigration issue. There are many ways to practice hospitality. We can begin by being generous with and practicing charity toward our friends and neighbors. But we cannot and must not end there! The Christian practice of hospitality must go beyond family, acquaintances, and even fellow citizens. Genuine hospitality reaches out to those we do not yet know, particularly to the immigrants who are in our midst and at our borders. By extending ourselves to these vulnerable ones we might not only entertain angels but actually meet Christ face to face.

The biblical command of being kind, merciful, and hospitable to immigrants is binding for everyone, from individuals, to institutions, to society as a whole. Christians are invited to establish a "culture of welcome" in their communities, without prejudices and biases and without making any distinction among the migrants because of nationality, color, or creed. In short, the Church is called to be a welcoming and peaceful meeting place, a "catholic" home for all.

Notes

1. International Organization for Migration (IOM), "World Migration Report 2018," available from https://www.iom.int/wmr/world-migration-report-2018 (accessed on April 2, 2020). See also https://migrationdataportal.org/data?i=stock_abs_&t=2019 (accessed June 30, 2020).

2. Timothy A. Lenchak, SVD, "Israel's Ancestors as Gerim: A Lesson of Biblical Hospitality," in *God's People on the Move: Biblical and Global Perspectives on Migration and Mission* (eds. văn Thanh Nguyễn and John M. Prior; Eugene, OR: Pickwick, 2014), 18-28.

3 https://www.un.org/en/development/desa/population/migration/publications/others/docs/toolkit_DESA_June%202012.pdf (accessed May 19, 2020).

4 https://www.un.org/en/development/desa/population/migration/publications/populationfacts/docs/MigrationStock2019_PopFacts_2019-04.pdf (accessed May 19, 2020).

5. https://madeintoamerica.org/child-immigrant-from-columbia-becomes-pr-pro/.

6. http://ratnaghosa.fwbo.net/danatwo.html (accessed May 19, 2020).

7. https://sf-hrc.org/what-human-trafficking (accessed July 15, 2020).

8. https://www.unitas.ngo/human-trafficking-101 (accessed July 16, 2020).

9. Marion L. S. Carson, *Setting the Captives Free: The Bible and Human Trafficking* (Eugene, OR: Cascade Books, 2015).

10. https://www.unhcr.org/en-us/news/stories/2020/5/5ecf78874/unhcr-helps-displaced-syrian-armenians-facing-hardship-amid-pandemic.html (accessed July 24, 2020).

11. https://www.unhcr.org/en-us/figures-at-a-glance.html (accessed July 10, 2020).

12. https://www.unhcr.org/en-us/rohingya-emergency.html (accessed July 9, 2020).

13. For the 2019 Africa Report on Internal Displacement prepared by the Internal Displacement Monitoring Centre (IDMC), see https://www.internal-displacement.org/sites/default/files/publications/documents/201912-Africa-report.pdf#page=16 (accessed June 20, 2020).

14. See https://www.unhcr.org/en-us/news/stories/2019/2/5c6139e74/nigerian-refugees-struggle-aftermath-boko-haram-attacks.html (accessed July 22, 2020).

15. https://www.unhcr.org/en-us/news/press/2020/6/5ee9db2e4/1-cent-humanity-displaced-unhcr-global-trends-report.html (accessed June 24, 2020).

16. https://www.unhcr.org/en-us/internally-displaced-people.html (accessed June 24, 2020).

17. https://peacekeeping.un.org/en/terminology (accessed July 23, 2020).

18. https://www.unhcr.org/en-us/climate-change-and-disasters.html (accessed July 28, 2020).

19. https://www.internal-displacement.org/global-report/grid2020/ (accessed July 28, 2020).

20. https://www.crs.org/stories/famine-threatens-east-africa (accessed July 29, 2020).

21. https://www.cnn.com/2020/04/22/africa/coronavirus-famine-un-warning-intl/index.html (accessed July 29, 2020).

22. https://www.wfp.org/news/wfp-chief-warns-hunger-pandemic-covid-19-spreads-statement-un-security-council (accessed August 3, 2020).

23. https://news.cornell.edu/stories/2017/06/rising-seas-could-result-2-billion-refugees-2100 (accessed July 29, 2020).

24. http://www.vatican.va/content/francesco/en/encyclicals/documents/papa-francesco_20150524_enciclica-laudato-si.html (accessed August 1, 2020).

25. vănThanh Nguyễn, SVD, "Migration in the New Testament: The Quest for Home," in *Christian Theology in the Age of Migration: Im-*

plications for World Christianity (ed. Peter C. Phan; Lanham, MD: Lexington Books, 2020), 69-84.

26   http://www.vatican.va/roman_curia/pontifical_councils/migrants/documents/rc_pc_migrants_doc_20040514_erga-migrantes-caritas-christi_en.html (accessed July 27, 2020).

27.   https://www.ucanews.com/news/child-brides-a-cover-for-cultural-pedophilia/78815 (accessed August 1, 2020).

28.   https://www.unicef.org/media/files/Child_Marriage_Report_7_17_LR..pdf (accessed August 1, 2020).

29.   https://www.unwomen.org/en/news/stories/2013/3/child-marriages-39000-every-day-more-than-140-million-girls-will-marry-between-2011-and-2020 (accessed August 5, 2020).

30.   https://migrationdataportal.org/themes/gender-and-migration (accessed August 8, 2020).

31.   https://globalfundforchildren.org/story/two-words-we-want-all-migrant-children-to-hear/?gclid=EAIaIQobChMIop-E5NCP-6wIVDb7ACh2r3weMEAAYASAAEgIpUvD_BwE (accessed August 5, 2020).

32.   https://www.unicef.org/emergencies/rohingya-beyond-survival-alert (accessed August 8, 2020).

33.   https://migrationdataportal.org/themes/child-and-young-migrants (accessed August 1, 2020).

34   https://www.poetryfoundation.org/poems/44266/mending-wall (accessed August 16, 2020).

35   https://www.usatoday.com/story/news/world/2018/05/24/border-walls-berlin-wall-donald-trump-wall/553250002/ (accessed August 16, 2020).

36   https://www.washingtonpost.com/immigration/trump-floating-border-wall/2020/08/14/fc42d0aa-dda3-11ea-b4af-72895e22941d_story.html (accessed August 16, 2020).

37   This subtitle is taken from a children's song called, "Joshua Fought the Battle of Jericho." See https://www.youtube.com/watch?v=Hu7mJElpE1Y (accessed August 16, 2020).

38 https://www.theatlantic.com/international/archive/2019/04/real-immigration-crisis-people-overstaying-their-visas/587485/ (accessed August 25, 2020).

39 https://www.cnn.com/2016/02/18/politics/pope-francis-trump-christian-wall/index.html (accessed August 19, 2020).

40 https://www.americamagazine.org/faith/2019/03/31/pope-francis-build-bridges-not-walls (accessed August 19, 2020).

41. https://www.pewresearch.org/fact-tank/2020/08/20/key-findings-about-u-s-immigrants/ (accessed August 26, 2020).

42. https://www.brookings.edu/policy2020/votervital/how-many-un-documented-immigrants-are-in-the-united-states-and-who-are-they/ (accessed August 26, 2020).

43. https://www.whitehouse.gov/briefings-statements/president-donald-j-trump-taking-action-ensure-american-citizens-receive-proper-representation-congress/ (accessed August 26, 2020).

44. For a definition of open borders and the pros and cons of this debate, see https://www.thoughtco.com/open-borders-4684612 (accessed September 3, 2020).

45. https://www.npr.org/sections/thetwo-way/2017/01/25/511565740/trump-expected-to-order-building-of-u-s-mexico-wall-wednesday (accessed August 29, 2020).

46. https://www.usccb.org/issues-and-action/human-life-and-dignity/immigration/strangers-no-longer-together-on-the-journey-of-hope (accessed August 29, 2020).

47. https://ignatiansolidarity.net/blog/2014/11/06/pope-francis-11/ (accessed August 29, 2020).

48. https://www.bushcenter.org/publications/resources-reports/reports/immigration.html (accessed September 1, 2020).

49. https://www.adl.org/resources/fact-sheets/myths-and-facts-about-immigrants-and-immigration-en-espanol?gclid=EAIaIQobChMIody29JLB6wIV0cDACh0fcQMnEAAYASAAEgLW6fD_BwE (accessed August 29, 2020).

50. M. Daniel Carroll R., *The Bible and Borders: Hearing God's Word on Immigration* (Grand Rapids, MI: Brazos Press, 2020), 64-72.

51. https://www.thedivinemercy.org/articles/top-10-mercy-quotes-pope-francis (accessed August 31, 2020).

52. https://faithmag.com/mercy-love-transformed (accessed August 31, 2020).

53. For the religious composition of internal migrants in 2010, see http://www.statista.com/statistics/221157/religious-composition-of-international-migrants/ (accessed August 2, 2020). See also http://www.pewforum.org/2012/03/08/religious-migration-exec/ (accessed August 2, 2020).

54. For charts and other pertinent statistics, see http://www.statista.com/statistics/221384/immigration-to-north-america-by-religion/ (accessed August 3, 2020).

55. See văn Thanh Nguyễn, "Migrants as Missionaries: The Case of Priscilla and Aquila," *Mission Studies* 30 (2013): 192-205.

56. Pontifical Council for the Pastoral Care of the Migrants and Itinerant People, "Starting Afresh from Christ: Towards a Renewed Pastoral Care for Migrants and Refugees." Fifth World Congress on the Pastoral Care of Migrants and Refugees (Rome, 2003) Part II, Pastoral Care, number 9. http://www.vatican.va/roman_curia/pontifical_councils/migrants/documents/rc_pc_migrants_doc_2004001_Migrants_Vcongress_%20findoc_en.html (accessed July 9, 2020).

57. https://www.usccb.org/committees/pastoral-care-migrants-refugees-travelers/welcoming-stranger-among-us-unity-diversity#conclusion (accessed July 9, 2020).

58. Asian and Pacific Presence: Harmony in Faith, number 1. Online: http://www.usccb.org/issues-and-action/cultural-diversity/asian-pacific-islander/resources/upload/AP-Pastoral-Statement-English.pdf (accessed January 10, 2018).

New City Press

New City Press is one of more than 20 publishing houses sponsored by the Focolare, a movement founded by Chiara Lubich to help bring about the realization of Jesus' prayer: "That all may be one" (John 17:21). In view of that goal, New City Press publishes books and resources that enrich the lives of people and help all to strive toward the unity of the entire human family. We are a member of the Association of Catholic Publishers.

www.newcitypress.com
202 Comforter Blvd.
Hyde Park, New York

Periodicals
Living City Magazine
www.livingcitymagazine.com

Scan to join our mailing list
for discounts and promotions
or go to www.newcitypress.com
and click on "join our email list."

Also available

WDBSA Friendship
Laurie Brink, O.P.
Paperback   978-1-56548-693-5

What does the Bible say about Friendship makes two extraordinary claims: that our life's ultimate goal is friendship with God and that our own personal friendships provide the road map.

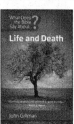

WDBSA Life and Death
John Gillman
Paperback   978-1-56548-405-4

The desire to live an abundant life and to have a good death remains a very contemporary aspiration for all of us in the twenty-first century. This resource addresses that desire as well as the complexities around such pressing issues as martyrdom, abortion, suicide, and capital punishment. The discussion includes references to official church statements as well as to current authors.

WDBSA Old Age
Ronald D. Witherup, P.S.S.
Paperback   978-1-56548-695-9

Have you ever wondered what the Bible says about growing old? This book deals directly with this timeless question that affects most human beings, especially in modern times.

WDBSA Forgiveness
Mary Ann Getty
Paperback   978-1-56548-407-8

Do we really know what the Bible says about forgiveness? Perhaps we think we do. The Bible's teaching, though, is more complex than we might imagine.